# Taking Leave

**Practices**

A series edited by Margret Grebowicz

*Fly-Fishing* by Christopher Schaberg
*Juggling* by Stewart Lawrence Sinclair
*Raving* by McKenzie Wark
*Riding* by Pardis Mahdavi
*Running* by Lindsey A. Freeman
*Taking Leave* by Deborah Kapchan
*Tomorrowing* by Terry Bisson

# Taking Leave

Deborah Kapchan

DUKE UNIVERSITY PRESS
*Durham and London*
2025

© 2025 DEBORAH ANNE KAPCHAN
*All rights reserved*
Project Editor: Liz Smith
Designed by A. Mattson Gallagher
Typeset in Untitled Serif and General Sans
by Copperline Book Services

Library of Congress Cataloging-in-Publication Data
Names: Kapchan, Deborah A. (Deborah Anne), author.
Title: Taking leave / Deborah Kapchan.
Other titles: Practices.
Description: Durham : Duke University Press, 2025. | Series:
Practices | Includes bibliographical references.
Identifiers: LCCN 2025004919 (print)
LCCN 2025004920 (ebook)
ISBN 9781478032823 (paperback)
ISBN 9781478029366 (hardcover)
ISBN 9781478061588 (ebook)
Subjects: LCSH: Kapchan, Deborah A. (Deborah Anne) |
Kapchan, Deborah A. (Deborah Anne)—Religion. | Muslim
converts—United States—Biography. | Sufi meditations. |
affect theory | LCGFT: Autobiographies.
Classification: LCC BP170.5 .K373 2025 (print) |
LCC BP170.5 (ebook) | DDC 297.8/14092 [B]—dc23/eng/20250515
LC record available at https://lccn.loc.gov/2025004919
LC ebook record available at https://lccn.loc.gov/2025004920

Cover text handwritten by Deborah Kapchan.

*for those in my life*
*who have taken their leave,*
*and yet remain . . .*

## CONTENTS

## A NOTE ON ORTHOGRAPHY

In deference to the orthographic practices of the religions I discuss here, I drop the /o/ from the word G-d, and follow the Prophet Muhammad's name with /pbuh/—"peace be upon him."

## PROLOGUE

And Jesus, walking by the sea of Galilee, saw two brethren, Simon called Peter, and Andrew his brother, casting a net into the sea: for they were fishers. And he saith unto them, Follow me, and I will make you fishers of men. And they straightway left their nets, and followed him.

—**Matthew 4:18–20**, King James

*IHVH-Adonaï dit à Abrâm:*
*"Va vers* toi, *de ta terre, de ton enfantement, de la maison de ton père, vers la terre que je te ferai voir."*

YHWH-Adonai said to Abram:
"Go towards *you*, from your land, from your birth, from your father's house, towards the land that I will show you."

—**Genesis 12:1**, Chouraqui translation, emphasis mine

I am sitting on a bench in a cemetery outside the Huguenot Memorial Church where I've just spent an hour with other ten-year-olds around a small Formica table, blue, green, red, and yellow pencils scattered before us, the odor of graphite, wood shavings, and Elmer's glue in the air. I'd been coloring in the outlines of a robed man motioning to some fishermen getting ready to set out to sea. The words "Follow me" were on the top of the white page, but the ones that reverberated the most were those that came after, "And they straightway left their nets." They took their leave.

I'm too young to understand the symbolism of those nets —the nets of ambition, of compulsion to work, to have a family, the nets of addiction, and other nets that entrap humans in suffering—but I know even then that I don't want to be caught in those snares. Rather I want the peace I experience when breathing in the moist soil and old stone of this cemetery. Is it the spirit of some long-dead saint buried there that is communicating with me?

I sit in that charnel ground, waiting for my father—not G-d, but the one of flesh and blood, the person I call my "real father" when I am with my friends, the one that picks me up every weekend from the garden apartment in New Rochelle where I live with my mother and her new husband.

My father Marvin would drive down the Pelham Parkway in his Ford station wagon on his one day off a week, a Jew from the Bronx traveling to the suburbs to pick up his daughter and take her back to 196th Street. Sometimes, after a lunch of fried chicken and potatoes with my immigrant grandfather, my grandmother in her slippers at the stove, my father took me to the zoo. We'd linger in the fusty elephant house, where

I'd put a quarter in the crank machine, receiving a handful of brown pellets in my palm to hold under their wet hairy trunks. Sometimes we'd take a drive to Old Bethpage to visit the cousins, stopping for hot bagels and splitting one on the spot. In an old sepia photograph my father wears a cashmere coat and a Stetson hat on a city street. He listened to jazz and read Lao-Tzu, or so he tells me later. What he doesn't tell me is that he was once drafted to fight in the Korean War and came back early, a pacifist with a junk habit. He would beat it, with the help of his Hungarian mother, Stella, and subsequently accede to her wishes: taking over the family business and becoming a kosher butcher. Not a glamorous job, but he'd compensate for the long hours, the sawdust floors, the bloodied aprons, and the lingering smell of tallow by pursuing my mother, a pretty blonde dancer from New England, and a goya.

My mother turns down a job as a Rockette to marry my father, and that soon becomes her biggest regret. When she goes back to work two years after I am born, it is at the Arthur Murray Dance Studios on Fordham Road in the Bronx. It is 1960. She wears four-inch heels and teases up her blonde hair, teaching cha-cha, foxtrot, waltz, and jitterbug to lonely men in baggy suits who want to lure women like her into their lives. But one man in particular draws her attention. Thomas Venute is the studio's manager, a tall, handsome con man straight out of an Arthur Miller novel. She will soon see the third-degree burns that cover most of his torso and left arm, the result of playing with matches in his pajamas as a child. (The priest came to the hospital five times to give him last rites, but little Tommy refused to die, going on to wear long-sleeve shirts for the rest of his life, even on the hottest days of summer.) He drinks martinis

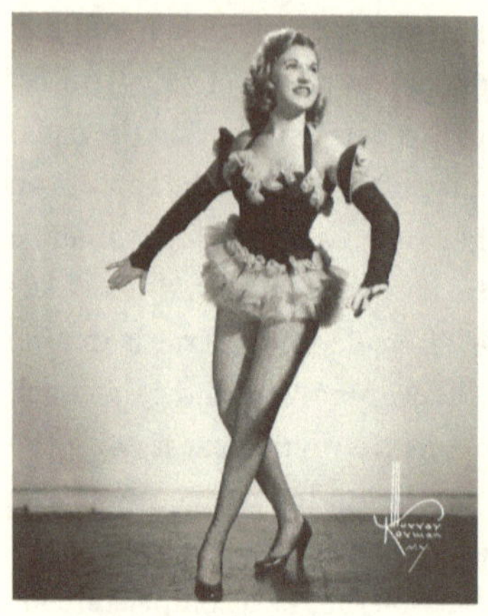

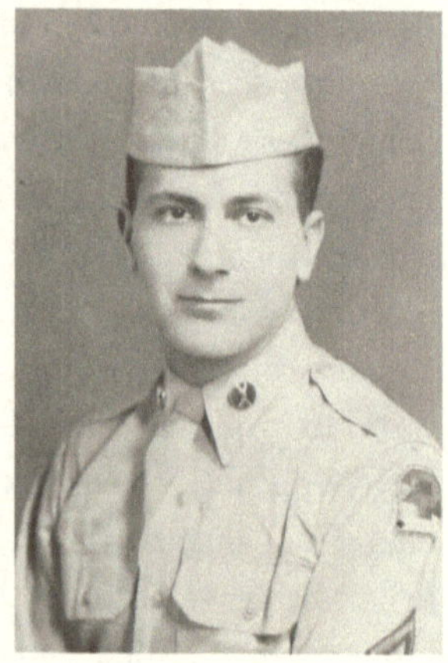

1 Nancy at age nineteen in her audition photograph for the Rockettes. (Photo: Author's Family Archives)

2 Marvin before going to Korea. (Photo: Author's Family Archives)

that I will learn to make for him ("just a liiiiitle bit of vermouth, Debbie doll"), and he gambles compulsively. He is, however, a great dancer. In a very short time, my mother divorces my father, and we all go on to live, if not the American dream, then an American drama.

My mother's leave-taking when I am just a baby suits my Jewish grandmother just fine. She never wanted her only son to marry a shiksa in the first place. Even if my mother *has* done the mikvah and converted to Judaism just to please her, she remains a White Anglo-Saxon Protestant in my grandmother's eyes; it is her birthright. Judaism is not. Stella paid for my mother's plane ticket to Tijuana, where she got a quick divorce.

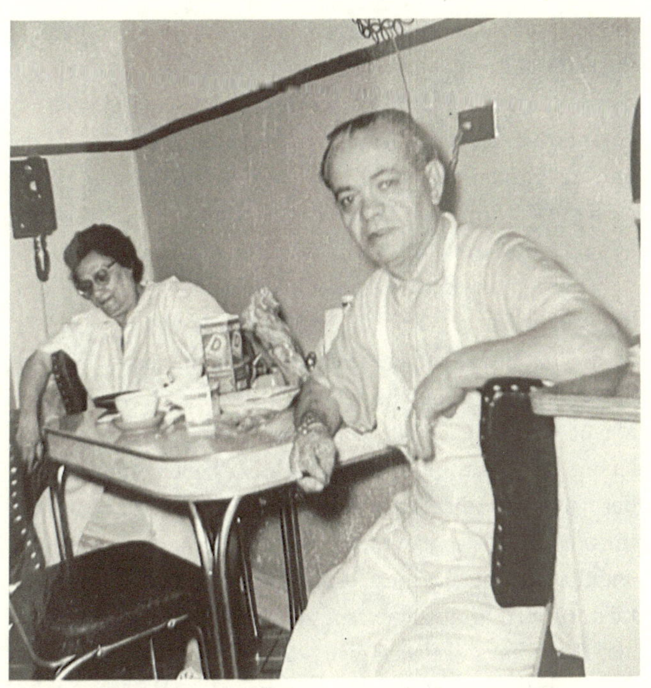

3 Stella and Nat, the author's grandparents, at the Formica table in the kitchen of their Bronx apartment. (Photo: Author's Family Archives)

This information is necessary at the get-go, as all leave-taking is a leaving *from*. And all leaving, including my own, is motivated. But not all people *take* their leave. Leave-taking is an act of volition, a deliberate possession of one's own departure, a conscious abstention from what is often called fate. It contains a paradox, as the etymology of *leave* is, in fact, "to remain." From the Old English *læfan* (to allow to remain in the same state or condition), taking leave is also a staying in place, a pause in time and space that allows something else to emerge. To take one's leave is to find home in a perpetually moving "residence on earth," to invoke Pablo Neruda. *Va vers toi et quitter la maison de ton père*. . . . Go toward your *self* and leave the house of your father. Or fathers in my case.

That Sunday in the cemetery is an aberration in our routine, as my father's usual day off is Saturday, the Jewish Sabbath. That he is picking me up after church means that he is not working at the butcher shop as usual. It is a Jewish holiday. Maybe Sukkot. He is late, but perhaps my Sunday school has let out early. I sit there on the cold stone bench, not thinking, but being, breathing. And somehow I know. I know that our time on earth is about stories, and that humans create them, and that writing one consciously is what matters, that the details are fairly arbitrary except that they are one's own. I know also that what will always give those stories impetus is in that very charnel ground. It is the presence of death. I do not find that morbid. It's not physical death I am sensing at the time, but the death before death that, I later learn, is a theme in all human myths, particularly the ones I'll go on to explore—those I inherited and those of my soon-to-be adopted homes in Morocco and France.

# Taking Leave

"WHAT RELIGIOUS HOLIDAYS do you celebrate?"

Airport security opens my passport. "Where do you live? Do you speak Hebrew? Have you been affiliated with any communities in the US or abroad?" I notice the Chabad booth a few meters from the check-in line, and a large poster of the Jewish mystic Rabbi Schneerson, next to two young men in black coats, ritual tassels dangling on each hip, *payot* curling from each side of their cheeks. Shouldn't JFK Airport be a secular space?

"My mother is Christian, my father is Jewish," I answer, omitting the fact that I have been practicing Sufi Islam for the last thirty years, and that my ex-husband is Moroccan, the socialist kind. "I celebrate everything."

The security woman looks at me suspiciously.

"I am an ecumenical," I clarify, drawing from the Greek *oikoumené*, one with "the inhabited earth."

"A what? What's that?"

"I'm secular."

I've changed my script and triggered the warning signals, so she goes to get her supervisor. It probably doesn't help that I have a residency visa for the United Arab Emirates in my passport, having lived in the capital of Abu Dhabi for the last five years.

I think about what they will find if they google me: publications about rites of passage and mystical rituals in Morocco and France, the possession ceremonies of the Gnawa, a sub-Saharan population in North Africa who propitiate the spirits, or jinn, with music and trance. I think that anodyne, but will they? I was told by a friend that, after journalists, academics are the most harassed people at the borders, and that's who they think I am. It says so on my visa for the UAE: "University Professor," though for me, that's only ever been my day job.

I am about to get on a flight to Tel Aviv. It is my first trip to Israel, and I'm flying El Al since their business class prices are the cheapest on the market, and with reason. Many of my friends now boycott everything Israeli, including El Al. They are signatories of BDS, the Boycott, Divestment, Sanctions movement in support of Palestine. Judith Butler, Cornel West, Brian Eno, and the late John Berger are also on the list, along with thousands of others. In fact, I am told that those who have signed the document have trouble getting into Israel at all. And yet I'm having trouble without having signed.

I am taken to a small room and seated on a gray plastic chair while they search my carry-on. I watch as the Israeli security policewoman takes out each object: a book by the French-Algerian Jewish author André Chouraqui called *Lettre à un Ami Arab*, my computer, phone cords, lip gloss. There are letters from Camille, my long-deceased mentor when I was seventeen and lived in France, as well as my mother's death certificate. She died less than a month ago. Now I take her with me in memory, along with the notebooks and papers I'd left with her for decades while I lived my nomadic life. I am taking these belongings to my ultimate destination, my "home" in Abu Dhabi, an archipelago on the edge of an orange-duned desert.

The island among islands where I live in the Gulf is landscaped with palm trees, white-flowering frangipani, holy basil, and paper-like petals of bougainvillea in yellow, orange, and fuchsia. My terrace looks over an estuary, rimmed with mangroves, their roots pushing up like eyed tendrils to the sun. It is here, between the mangal mud and the green-blue water of the lagoon, that I have chosen to write about my intertidal existence.

Perhaps it's my mother's dream that has taken up residence inside me now. My mother always wanted to go to the "Holy Land," and when I tell her just a few months before her death that I have been invited to speak in Jerusalem, she once again expresses this desire. Instead of indulging her and saying, "Maybe one day, Mom," I am short and impatient. "Do you have ten thousand dollars, Mom? Because that's what it will cost." I know she thinks I have that kind of spare cash, but I don't. Or at least not now. I don't want to be dependent on *my* kids when I am in my eighties. I need to save money for the visiting nurses and care that she hasn't been able to afford. And in any case, she can no longer walk, and cataracts have clouded her eyes. It is difficult for me to watch her demise. She knows this. Still, she says, "Deborah, when did you get so hard? Why are you so impatient with me?"

It's true. I am. Or was. And not only with my mother but also with my children, and particularly with my son. But that's because I know he will forgive me, while I fear my daughter Hannah may not. She is half-Amazigh (or Berber), the indigenous people of North Africa, the people in Morocco before all the colonizers came—the Carthaginians, the Romans, the

Vandals, the Arabs, and most recently the Spanish and the French. In addition to her Amazigh bloodline, my daughter's DNA test shows Arab and African roots on her father's side. On mine, she is a quarter northern European and a quarter Ashkenazi. My daughter, now a therapist, has cultivated firm boundaries so as not to let my biting Jewish sarcasm get under her skin.

When I call her and say, "Grandmom has passed," she asks me to repeat myself. She doesn't think she's heard correctly. We thought she'd live longer than eighty-seven years. Perhaps that's because my mother denied the possibility of death until the very end. She died in my arms in a motel in Woods Hole, Massachusetts, where she, my twenty-year-old son Nathaniel, and I stopped for the night, on our road trip to Maine, the place my mom spent her happiest days. We were taking her home one last time.

My mother always wanted to visit Jerusalem, to walk where Jesus walked. But it was an article I wrote on my paternal *Jewish* roots that has landed me at JFK in a room where they are now searching my bags. The article was read by an esteemed colleague at Hebrew University, an activist and a poet, who invited me to give a talk at her institution. I will not discuss the article, however. No, I will talk about my most recent book, an anthology of Moroccan poetry. I will talk about translation and how decades of living in Morocco sensitized me to the sediment of orality that underlies the written word. I will not talk about the thirty years I have spent in a Sufi order there, or the way my Judaism haunts everything that came before and would come after: the three religions of the book that live in me like breath.

I am finally ushered forward toward security, standing with Jewish families, including a group taking their adolescent daughters to yeshiva in Israel. A short heavyset woman is going up and down the line, checking off their names on her clipboard. It's 2023. Women as well as men are encouraged to study the Torah. A trim couple ahead of me are dressed in conservative black. The woman, in a long skirt and stylish beret, holds a toddler. I look at the baby and try to make him smile, realizing I am the age of his grandmother, the nice older lady traveling alone to Israel. Could that possibly be me? The father is noticeably excited to be bringing his eldest daughter to the Holy Land, where he will leave her to study, a rite of passage, a new chapter. All four of their children are well behaved, and I envy the assuredness of this attractive couple, who, I imagine, know who they are: New York Jews of a certain professional class, raising a family and upholding the traditions of their forebears. No divorce. No domestic abuse. Or so I fantasize.

And where and who am I on this line?

I am the daughter of a shiksa, the first grandchild not to go to Hebrew School and be bat mitzvahed, despite the fact that Stella, my Hungarian grandmother, insisted my mother do the mikvah and convert before the wedding. My mother, Nancy, ceded to her future mother-in-law's wishes, submerging her svelte dancer's body in the pool while a hefty woman with a *shmatta* on her head said the Hebrew prayers before each dunk:

*Barukh atah Adonay Eloheynu melekh ha-olam . . .*

Nancy took a deep breath and went under, squeezing her lids tightly against the warm water. "Our father who art in heaven . . ." she began in silent counterpoint. But she had to come up for air before she finished.

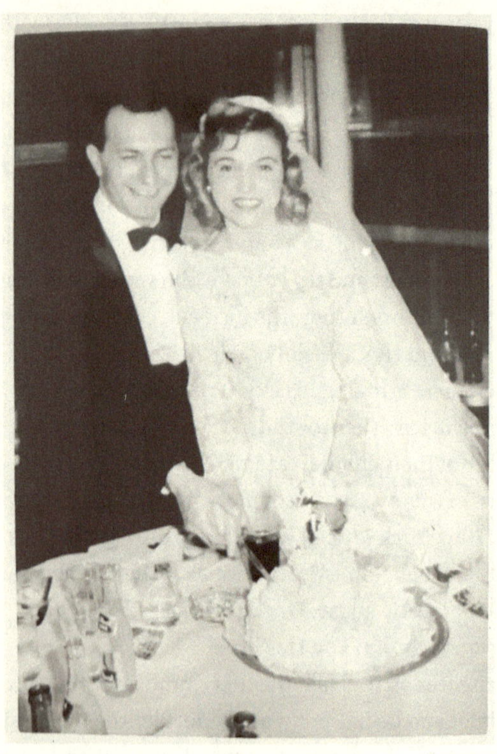

**4** The couple after their Christian wedding, April 1957. (Photo: Author's Family Archives)

*Barukh atah Adonay, Eloheynu melekh ha-olam* . . .

She went under again. "Forgive me Jesus, forgive me Jesus," she intoned sotto voce as the thick arm pulled her back up.

*V'eyrastikh li, l'olam. V'eyratikh li b'tzedek u'v'mishpat* . . . "I will betroth you to me, forever. I will betroth you to me with righteousness and with justice, with goodness and

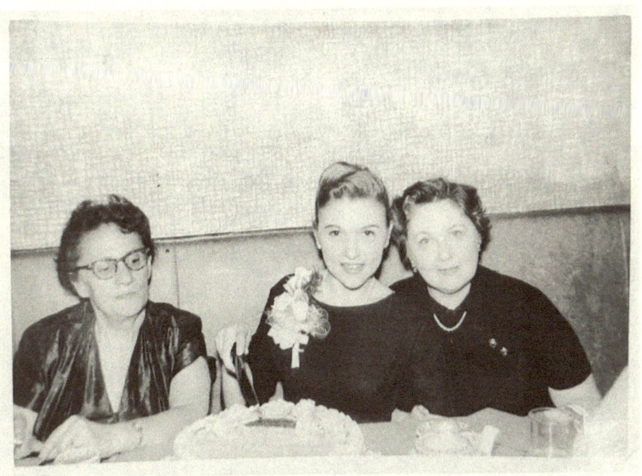

5 Marriage celebration at a Chinese restaurant in New York, April 1957. Nancy (*center*) with her Jewish Hungarian mother-in-law, Stella (*left*), and her Christian Swedish mother, Thelma (*right*), after the Jewish wedding ceremony. (Photo: Author's Family Archives)

with compassion. I will betroth you to me in truth, and we will come to know G-d."

She emerged one final time, purified of her past and one with the waters of Judaism.

My mother never practiced, never learned to make latkes or matzah-ball soup. And as if to compensate for the heresy of conversion, her Christian faith only grew stronger as she aged. She worried about my soul out loud more than once.

And here I stand now, with hundreds of New York Jews, my mother in the ground, and me about to take off, to take what might be my final leave to a place I never wanted to go,

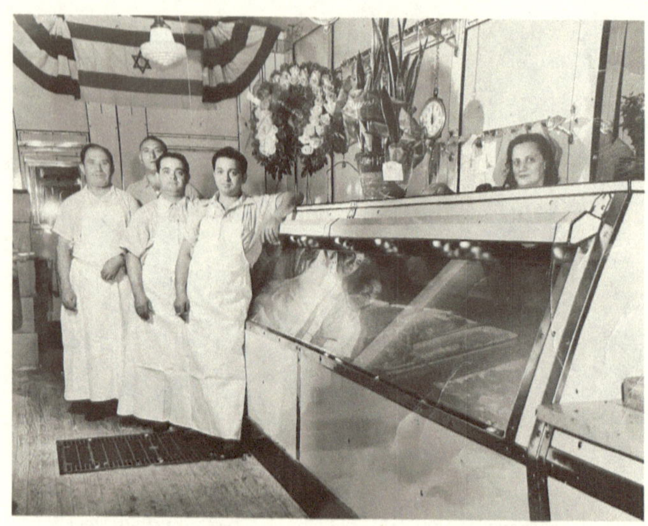

6 Opening day at the kosher butcher shop in the Bronx. From the left, two unidentified employees, the author's grandfather Nathan Kapchan, his brother Harry Kapchan, and the author's grandmother Stella behind the counter. (Photo: Author's Family Archives)

with people, a people, I do not know, but who always seem to recognize me.

Airports are liminal spaces, "non-places" Marc Augé calls them. Everyone is on their way to somewhere else. Taking leave. Perhaps this is why I am so comfortable in these halls, though the long security lines and crowds bother me more and more as time passes. Still, I walk through the high-ceilinged terminal

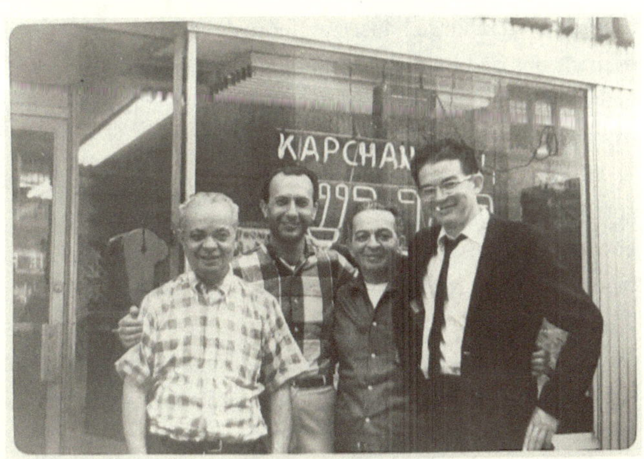


**7** Kapchan and Son, Kosher Butchers. Nathan Kapchan, Marvin Kapchan, Harry Kapchan, and his son Paul Kapchan. (Photo: Author's Family Archives)

thinking of all the other leave-takings that have held me aloft like a sponge in an airy sea.

The first time I took a plane by myself, I was just seventeen and going to France. I had applied to be the study-abroad student representing my high school, but that hadn't worked. The evening the committee of bourgeois ladies came to interview my parents (my drunken stepfather deliberately not home), my mother baked an apple pie. The committee sat on the faux baroque couch, the gold crushed-velvet upholstery under their tight bums, and asked why my mother thought her daughter was the right choice to be a cultural ambassador. I remember she talked about her Christian faith. I think she was "witnessing." At least half of them were Jewish and the rest were WASPs, but they all lived in large houses in Shore Acres, a neighborhood of mansions on Long Island Sound. They left, and I thought I heard them laughing as they got in their BMWs and pulled away from our rental apartment. I was mortified.

If I was going to get to Europe, I'd have to do it myself. So I got a job bringing burgers and fries to tables of suburban families every weekend, my sneakers sticking to the greasy floor of a diner, while a pretty classmate from the *right* side of the Boston Post Road went off to France. Undaunted, I counted my nickels, dimes, and quarters at the end of every shift and when I had eight hundred dollars, I quit and bought a plane ticket to France where I would spend the summer in a small village in the Massif Central. (The introduction to my host family was made by a French woman my mother had fortuitously met in a local park.)

I had expected to become friends with the children in the family. However, Isabelle and her brother were much younger than me. Instead, I spent the summer with their grandfather Docteur Camille, addressing him with the formal *vous* the whole time. We corresponded for years after that summer. His letters are with me now on this flight.

"This town is very old," Camille told me a few days after I arrived in La Creuse as we walked to the village café. He wore a sweater under his loose suit even in summer to cover his bone-thin frame. "The village church was built on the site of a pagan temple, you know. They wanted to bury all those influences. But they still live in the soil of this place. History doesn't disappear, it just goes underground."

"When did Christianity come to France?"

"That was a black day," Camille said, a glint in his eye. "Some Gauls were already Christianized in the second century. From that time on, there have just been wars. Protestants. Catholics. Nonstop conflicts."

"My grandmother's Swedish ancestors were French Huguenots," I said. "They went to Sweden during the religious wars."

"Ah, *bon*? But isn't Kapchan a Jewish name?"

"*Oui*. My father is Jewish, but I was brought up with my mother in the Protestant church. My parents divorced when I was young. My Jewish grandmother couldn't accept a Christian in the family."

"You see? Religion is just divisive," he said.

"Yes, but don't you believe in something greater than humans, an intelligence who made all this?"

"Stories," he said of my belief in a higher power. "Fairy tales. Of course, there's lots that we don't understand, but humans need to learn to live with uncertainty. I listen to science."

"I listen to science too," I said, repeating the sentence back to him like I did in French class, "but I think there's something spiritual we need to understand. I think there are mysteries."

Camille smiled at me. "You're a mystery," he said, as he opened the door of the café. "How is it that you arrived here in this little *patelin*?" He placed his hand on my shoulder and we exchanged a long glance. "But you're too young to be so serious." He winked, and I walked in.

"*Salamu-alay-kum*," Camille said to the man behind the cashier's desk.

"*Alay-kum salam*, Monsieur le Maire," he answered.

"I'll have a coffee, and Deborah, what, a *jus d'abricot*?" I nodded. Camille bought *Le Monde Diplomatique*, and we went outside to sit down.

I had so many questions. But we sat in the sun in peaceful silence while Camille read the headlines.

"You know, I was in North Africa when I was young," he said, looking up. "After medical school I went there as an intern. You could be Moroccan, Algerian, or Tunisian the way you look. Dark eyes, dark hair. There *are* North African Jews. They aren't all Muslim."

"I don't think I've ever met a Muslim," I said.

"No! Well, you just did! Mohamed, who sold us the paper, is a Muslim. His daughter is Isabelle's best friend."

Camille was once the village doctor, but when his daughter finished medical school and got married, he invited his son-in-law to share his practice. An office, which smelled of leather and isopropyl alcohol, connected their two residences. I took this passage frequently when lunches were at Camille's, passing glass jars of sterile cotton and papered examination tables. Now, however, Camille was the mayor of the village, attending regional meetings in Guéret, organizing cultural events and building a tourist center in town.

Camille told me about growing up in the Limousin region. He showed me pictures of himself as a boy with long locks of hair and a sash. He told me about his experiences as a *maquisard* in the Resistance, about the day the Germans came to the house looking for "Der Doktor" who was treating the wounded French resistance fighters. These stories fascinated me because they happened in these hills, in this village, in this house. And because Camille had put his life on the line trying to defeat the Nazi occupiers.

"I had no choice," he said, when I marveled at his bravery. "We had been invaded."

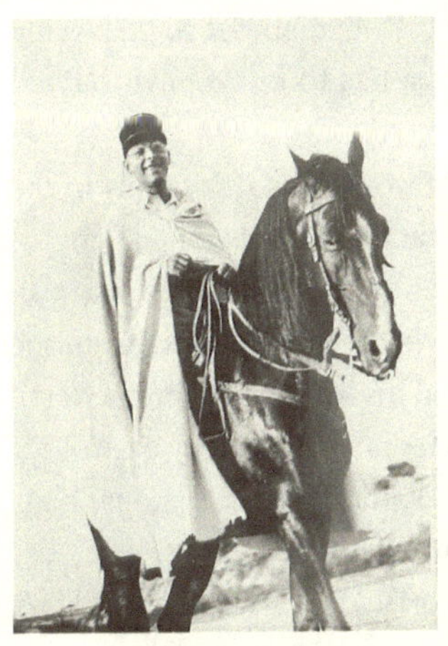
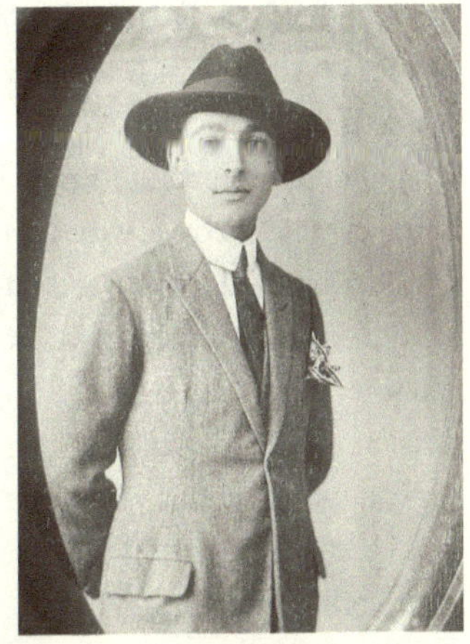

**8** Camille Aumasson on horseback, while doing his civil service in North Africa as a doctor. (Photo: Aumasson Family Archives, provided by Isabelle Granjean, b. Chaubier)

**9** Camille Aumasson, around age seventeen, in the Limousin region of France. (Photo: Aumasson Family Archives, provided by Isabelle Granjean, b. Chaubier)

But he came most alive when speaking of his experiences in Tunisia before World War II. He went there after medical school to do his *service civile* and fell in love with the country.

"Here I am in the desert treating the Bedouin," he said, showing me a sepia photograph.

"You're on a horse!"

"Yes, and wearing a burnoose. The sun and wind were brutal. And here I am back in the city." A young Camille stood in a white doctor's cloak in front of a building.

"What was your specialty?"

"I did whatever they needed, from diabetes to delivering babies. A doctor in North Africa has to know how to treat everything."

Upon his return to France he would raise his family in the same granite fortress where we sat together looking at photographs, their edges wedged under brown cardboard tabs in an album. And although it was a typical French house from the outside, Camille had transformed his living room into a North African salon, with low banquettes, a copper tray on wobbly legs, a metal teapot with a set of small filigree glasses. Flatweave kilims covered the cement-tile floor.

Was it Camille's fate to go to North Africa? Was it *al-maktub*, "written" for him? France was a colonial power at the time; it was easy to sit on a horse wearing a burnoose without thinking of the privileges this entailed. So many French fell in love with the colonies, the land, its people. But they lived in homes with running water and had servants.

Was it *al-maktub* that I came to the middle of France, to a place and a man whose melancholy echoed my own?

I remember clearly the day the two of us were sitting on the divan after lunch. Tipping the end of his cigarette into the metal ashtray, Camille asked me to follow him to his library. His white wool burnoose still hung on the coat rack in the corner. I stood there while he searched for a book among the medical manuals and literature.

"Ah, voilà," he said, pulling a small red leatherbound volume from the shelf. "Rumi. Do you know him?"

"*Non*," I said. "*Qui est-il?*"

"A very great poet. A philosopher, in fact. He was a Sufi."

"A what?"

"A Sufi. A mystic like you," he added. "He believed in synchronicity." He winked. "For Sufis, if you haven't lived it, it isn't true. Listen," he said, as he leafed through the pages with his yellowed fingers. "Here's one for the Protestant side of you." He broke into a wry smile.

> Lord, said David, since you do not need us,
> Why did you create these two worlds?
> Reality replied: O prisoner of time,
> I was a secret treasure of kindness and generosity,
> and I wished this treasure to be known,
> so I created a mirror: its shining face, the heart;
> its darkened back, the world;
> The back would please you if you've never seen the face.
> Has anyone ever produced a mirror out of mud and straw?
> Yet clean away the mud and straw,
> and a mirror might be revealed.
>
> Until the juice ferments a while in the cask,
> it isn't wine. If you wish your heart to be bright,
> you must do a little work.

Camille looked up at me, smiled, and took a drag on his Gauloise. I heard the tobacco leaves burning and the smoke entering his lungs. A small piece of cigarette paper clung to his bottom lip.

"We're prisoners of time," he said, his eyes squinting in affection. He squeezed my hand and held it in his for a long while.

"Here, take this back to the other house with you," he said, releasing his grip and breaking the spell.

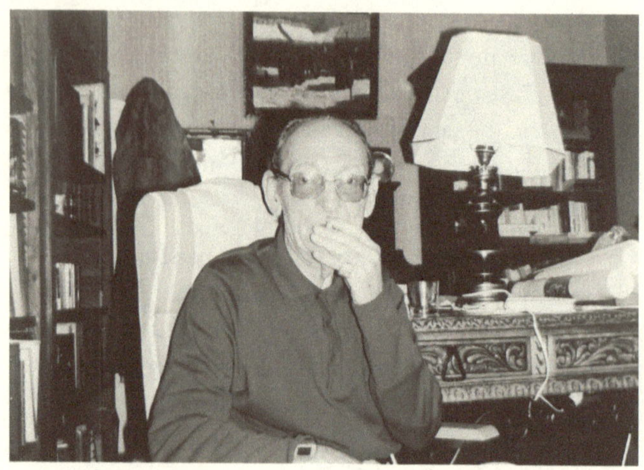

**10** Camille Aumasson at seventy-one, smoking a Gauloise filterless cigarette in his office in La Creuse. (Photo: Aumasson Family Archives, provided by Isabelle Granjean, b. Chaubier)

I accepted the book and left Camille to his siesta. Rumi was my French textbook for the rest of that summer.

Once on the plane, I open Chouraqui's book, *Letter to an Arab Friend*, and read about the Jerusalem of the character's youth, when he, an Algerian Jew, and his best friend, an Arab Muslim, moved freely between each other's homes, speaking their mutual natal language, Arabic. I underline these words:

> Sur les sommets, les poètes, les théologiens, les maîtres spirituels, s'exprimaient dans cette seule langue. Le Bible

hébraïque, le Talmud araméen, étaient enseigné en arabe, langue qui avait supplanté l'araméen et l'hébreu dans une vaste partie du monde Juif. Le style, c'est l'homme et la langue en est l'âme.

On the summits, poets, theologians, spiritual masters expressed themselves in this language alone. The Hebrew Bible, the Aramaic Talmud, were taught in Arabic, a language which had supplanted Aramaic and Hebrew in a large part of the Jewish world. Style is the man and language is his soul.

What travels in a language, a tongue? I think of the languages my in-laws spoke: Tamazight, Arabic, and French. Or my grandfather who spoke Yiddish, Russian, and, much later, broken English. A language for home, a language for the colonizer, a language to make one's way in realities other than one's own. A different language for a different way of being, a new perception; and *style*, in both language and life, carving out a form. Style, not in the sense of fashion, but a culture, a disposition, a taste, a way of being in one's skin while moving through the flesh of the world. Chouraqui, a lawyer and intellectual, went on to translate not only the Bible but the Qur'an into French.

I put the book in my lap and drift into the fugue state of transcontinental slumber, high above the politics of history on the ground.

When I land, I take a taxi directly to Jerusalem. I'm staying in the new city, in a hotel in the neighborhood of Rehavia. My room is not quite ready, so I leave my bag at the desk and sit outside in a nearby café, drinking a cappuccino, the September sun warming my face.

Women with wigs and ankle-length skirts walk by. Orthodox Jews, I think. Young women in bust-clinging tops and flowing skirts, with scarves falling loosely back from their hairlines, are their unmarried daughters. Men in jeans with yarmulkes and tzitzit are conservative; men in hats and black suits are Orthodox. Young women with short sleeves are secular. Older women with uncovered hair and pants are secular too but respectful of the cultural norms.

In a few hours, when I walk to the Jaffa Gate, I will see Muslim women, their hair tightly wrapped in one scarf while another is wound under their chins and then tied discreetly at the nape of their necks, their robes flowing long to the ground. I will see Muslim men in pastel djellabas of blue and beige walking to the mosque in traditional slippers and leather sandals, and young Palestinians, in jeans, much like the tourists, but somehow identifiable by their gait, by the way they inhabit their skin, hyperaware of their occupier's gaze. I will not be able to enter the old city, however, as police have put up a blockade. Three Orthodox Jews have just been stabbed, and I watch an ambulance careen them away.

The conference, it turns out, is about Jewish folklore. And while I will talk about poetry translation, my topic has been made to fit the bill. It seems I will give the last paper of the day, a guest lecture at four p.m. But at ten in the morning, there are many papers before mine, and they will all be in Hebrew. I listen assiduously, at least at first, bathing in the music of a language I don't know. Listening is what I do best. It is, in fact, what I write about: The Sufi ceremony of chanting is itself called "listening," *sama'*, perhaps because making a sound depends upon hearing it first, perhaps because attuning one's ear to the sounds of devotion creates an empathic connection to the divine. Every vibration has a sound, whether the human ear can hear it or not. It's the effort to listen—*samaa*—that opens the heart. When the ancients spoke of the music of the spheres, they were not far off the mark.

I am surprised by how soft Hebrew sounds to my ear—so unlike Moroccan Arabic, which shortens the long vowels of classical Arabic, rendering staccato what is mellifluous elsewhere in the Arab world. Yet I hear right away when a Palestinian scholar takes the floor. His Hebrew is more clipped, the consonants more pronounced. We are known by our styles, by the way we accent our words, though I think I recognize many Hebrew/Arabic cognates. Hebrew, I think, would not be too hard to learn.

"What does *pitgamim* mean?" I ask Galit after my talk. It was a word that was repeated over and over during the day.

"Very good," Galit said. "You understood." *Pitgam* means "proverb." It was the theme of most of the papers. And she quotes a proverb from the Bible. *Kno khokhmah mah tov mekharutz u-knot binah nivkhar mi-kasef.* How much better to get wisdom than gold, to choose understanding rather than silver (Proverbs 16:16).

The next day I accompany my hosts, Galit and Freddie, to the gates of Beit HaNassi, the residence of the president of Israel. They have been going there every Saturday evening for more than forty weeks to protest the policies and corruption of Netanyahu's government. We walk through a sea of hundreds of people, as Galit greets her brothers and sisters in arms, many founders of the Women in Black that have been protesting the occupation of the territories since the first Intifada in 1987. I buy a T-shirt that says, "No democracy without peace," and we listen to young people with microphones denouncing the Israeli government.

"How can you stay here," I ask Galit naively, "when you are against the occupation? There's so much tension in the air." I know that they have an apartment in Chicago where their daughter is a professor.

"Our presence is needed here," she responds. "As secular Jews who disagree with the policies of the government, we are a kind of conscience. What's more," she adds, "this energy, we've gotten used to it. It's hard to live anywhere else."

After the conference is over, I move to a hotel in the old city, just inside the Jaffa Gate. It is run by a Christian Palestinian family. When Avi, my guide, comes to the hotel the next morning, he tells me that the government wanted to confiscate the building, appropriate it, as they had so many other homes during the first Nakba, but that the family had won the legal case. Unusual. A large painting of a Catholic patriarch hangs in the lobby, his tall hat and long habit adorned with a conspicuous cross. I did not choose the hotel for its religious confession, did not even know. There would never be such stark affiliations declared in a hotel in New York. In France it would be scandalous. (In Morocco, it's the king's photo displayed in hotel lobbies; in Syria, before the fall of the regime, it was Assad's.) And yet here in Jerusalem there is no such thing as neutral. One is a Christian or a Muslim or a Jew (whether Orthodox or secular). And there are tourists of course, some undeclared, but many—like the group of African Americans on a church tour that checked in just before me—on religious pilgrimage.

When Avi arrives, we sit for a few minutes in the worn leather chairs in the cement-tiled lobby. He is personable and warm, about thirty, and has even read my work. We've already had a lively exchange by WhatsApp when I first contacted him two months ago. I was in New York then, and my mother was alive. He began to leave me voice messages in his lightly Hebrew-accented English. Not knowing then how very small the walled city of Jerusalem was, I asked him about our itinerary, where we'd go. I told him about my mixed heritage and about my thirty years of research with Moroccan Sufis. I wanted to see Jerusalem through the eyes of all three religions, I told him. It was then that he suggested that I also hire his friend Adam, a Christian guide, and his friend Ahmed, a Muslim, as well. Avi himself was recommended by a Jewish contact in the UAE. He is her friend, but also graduated from the two-year post-university program that certifies one to become an official tourist guide in Israel. Apparently, the training is stringent, with courses in history and language. Avi grew up in an ultra-Orthodox Jewish family but left the tradition in order to play a more integral role in society. I have three more days in Jerusalem, I tell him when he arrives, and I want to follow the stones of time, beginning with Judaism, the oldest of the three religions that share the one G-d.

We begin walking, and he tells me the history of Jerusalem's many conquerors and inhabitants: the Canaanites, the Romans, Constantine the Great of the Byzantine Empire, the Arab Umayyads and Abbasids under which all three religions of the book thrived. Later came the Seljuks and the Crusaders. I try to keep these straight in my mind, but the list of colonizers is long. After the Christians, the Ottomans ruled Jerusalem under Suleiman the Magnificent, from 1516 to 1918, a long stint, and one wherein religious freedom once again reigned. But when the Ottomans were defeated and the British Mandate proclaimed, it was the practice of divide and conquer that obtained. More Zionists came to what was then called Israel and further displaced the Palestinians.

Avi takes me down an alley.

"Not too many people know about this place," he tells me. "It's between the Muslim and the Orthodox Jewish Quarter, a few blocks where both Muslims and Jews share the very same streets." It's an ecotone, I think to myself, a region between two ecologies that shares elements of both but is neither.

We stand on the roof of what Avi says is a hammam, a Muslim public bath, and look across at the Jewish cemetery on the slope of the Mount of Olives. Avi tells me about the belief that those buried closest to the Temple will rise first and enter through the Lion's Gate to heaven. I learn that this same temple, built by King Solomon in the tenth century BCE and destroyed in 587 BCE by Nebuchadnezzar and then again in 70 CE by the Romans, lies below the Dome of the Rock, where Abraham was ready to sacrifice his son Isaac (or Ishmael for Muslims). Orthodox Jews will not visit that site, the holy of holies, until the Messiah comes; instead, they pray at the Western Wall that surrounds the sacred ground. The wall, a limen dividing inside from out, past from present, sacred from profane, Jew from Muslim.

"We'll go there next," he says. But before we can resume our tour, the muezzin calls the *dhuhr* prayer from a nearby mosque. Avi and I both pause, standing stock still, and listen to our bones, while a young Orthodox man walks quickly in front of us, over the roof to his neighborhood beyond.

In a few minutes I will leave Avi, cover my head, and pray at the women's section of the Western Wall, tears streaming from my eyes, for the soul of my recently dead mother, and for my father who died many years ago now. I will pray for the still-vibrant flesh of my children, that they stay safe and thrive, wedging a piece of paper with their names in a crevasse in the rock. There are hundreds, maybe thousands, of these white squares of writing angled into the wall and littering the ground. I imagine the person who collects them at the end of each day—or is it week or month?—sweeping up the supplications and taking them to their own burial place.

A genizah—from the Hebrew root, *g-n-z*, "to hide" or "to put away," and from Old Medean *ganza*, "depository; treasure"—is a repository for papers with the name of G-d on them, usually in the attic or basement of a synagogue, but sometimes in a designated building in a cemetery. A paper interment. A sacred archive. In Arabic it is related to جنازة, funeral. Is there a genizah for these daily discarded prayers?

I find Avi, and we continue our walk through the medina. The air is crisp this September morning, the sun warm. I am wearing an open cloak made of black raw silk, lined in a light celadon, over loose silk slacks, all tailored for me in Abu Dhabi. It's a diversion among me and my girlfriends there—buying fabric and having things custom made, something prohibitively expensive in Europe or the United States. And while there is no dress code for expats in Abu Dhabi, the predominance of Indian, Pakistani, and Arab fashion makes dressing in loose

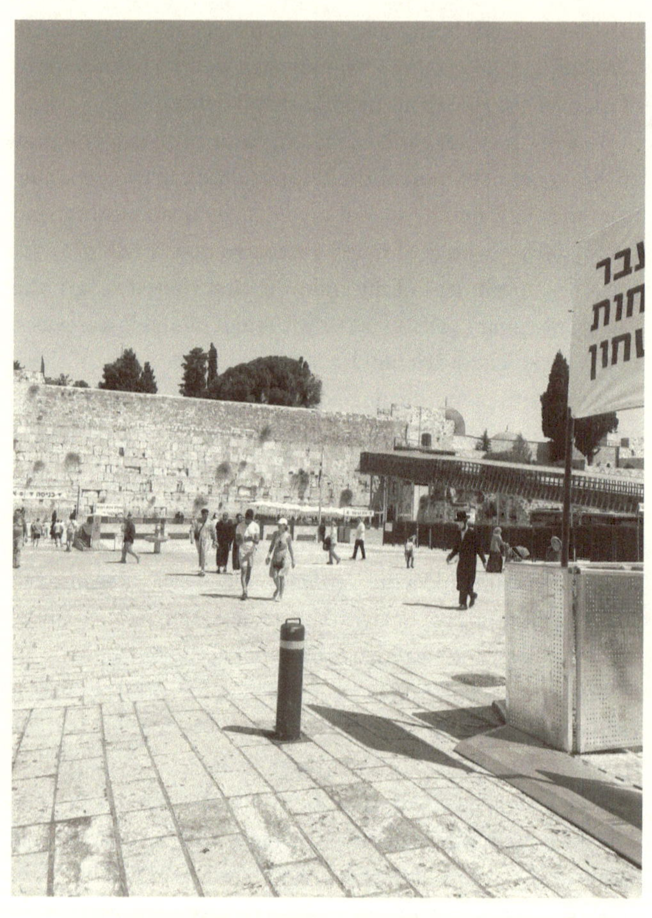

11 The Western Wall in Jerusalem. (Photo: Deborah Kapchan)

flowy clothes attractive. Sexual dimorphism is the rule of the game there. Emirati women wear impossibly high-heeled shoes under their abayas.

Avi has told me that it is better to cover when walking through the Jewish Quarter, that tourists in scanty dress are actually insulted there and sometimes solicit aggression. It's hard to imagine religious people doing such things, but then their neighborhood is constantly flooded with gawking tourists. I hope my garb allows a passe-partout, but there is no way I can pass as a local of any ilk. I don't even look American. At least I hope I do not.

We walk past ultra-Orthodox men in white stockings, their pants above their ankles, their prayer shawls over their shoulders, some with wool *shtreimels* on their heads, despite the warm weather. It's an image familiar to me—a half-Jew who, as an adult, spent some time living in a Brooklyn neighborhood just blocks from the borough's burgeoning Lubavitcher community. What's more, my grandfather came from a village in Ukraine not far from the birthplace of their founder, the mystic Baal Shem Tov, or Master of the Good Name, who exhorted his followers to find the divine immanent within. And yet, even if this may be part of my heritage, when I look at them, nothing signals *home*. That is a place I've yet to find, except perhaps in the spaces I inhabit when taking leave.

"This is the main street that goes to the mosque," Avi tells me, as we walk past vegetable stands overflowing with purple onions, carrots, and large slices of pumpkin, clothing merchants displaying colorful gandouras and scarves, and juice bars with fresh oranges and pomegranates piled high. The abundant scenery is familiar to me from years of living in the medinas of Marrakech and Fès. Nonetheless, Avi seems a bit surprised by my fluency in Arabic, though he has read my article and knows I've been practicing Sufism for many years. He also speaks fluent Arabic, and we converse a bit together, and then with a merchant who makes us a fresh glass of red juice that stains our lips.

"Let's take a break here," he tells me, pointing at a building across from where we're standing. "Soon the streets will be crowded with people coming back from the mosque."

I follow Avi up a set of polished stone stairs at the corner of the Via Dolorosa and al-Wad Street, and we enter the Austrian Hospice, a hostel for Christian pilgrims since 1863, with a chapel and a garden café serving apple strudel, of all things! Avi knows the concierge, who leaves his desk long enough to unlock the metal grate that leads up to the roof. We ascend the winding staircase, the only two people there.

"This is the best view around," Avi says to me when we reach the top. And indeed, all of Jerusalem lies before us—the Jewish Quarter to our left, the Dome of the Rock on the Temple Mount straight ahead. In the distance I can see the Dormition Abbey on Mount Zion. As we stand on the roof of the oldest Christian guest house in Jerusalem, I realize that the map of the old city, less than a square kilometer in all, is also a map of my history, a close proximity of Jew, Christian, and Muslim, the streets like the veins in my body, a cohabitation of traditions impossible to pull apart.

The outer circumstances of our lives always mirror an inner reality, I think to myself. And then the words "a house divided against itself cannot stand" come to mind. Where is that saying from? When I look it up later, I find it was Lincoln, quoting Jesus, who was being criticized. "But Jesus knew their thoughts, and said to them: Every kingdom divided against itself is brought to desolation, and every city or house divided against itself will not stand" (Matthew 12:25). Why is it so difficult to inhabit the spaces between the three religions of the book? Why is it that despite the similar characters in their stories, any one of these religions demands an exclusivity that goes counter to the love, acceptance, and peace they all eulogize? Is it a blessing or a curse to be able to inhabit different perspectives, to know in one's body the orientation of another language, another sacred culture? How can I reside in that multiplicity without falling apart, to be without belonging? Perhaps it's that question that led me to Islam, a religion with no claim on me, at least not one that I remembered.

I'm still not quite sure why I went down that path and not another. Yes, I had to write more books, to be an ethnographer, in order to retain my position as a professor at the University of Texas. I needed a project, but the one I proposed for my Fulbright year was about women's oral traditions and had nothing at all to do with religion. It was 1994, and I was living in a third-floor apartment in a bourgeois neighborhood in Rabat, the coastal capital of Morocco. My terrace looked over a long row of palm trees that lined the street, ending at the Tour Hassan Esplanade, with its mosque and its marble mausoleum for Mohammed the Fifth, Morocco's independence king. At dusk, the swifts would fly out of the fronds and circle the sky with insect-like frenzy, while the call to prayer sounded over the city from all sides.

I see it in my mind's eye. It is the *maghreb*, or sunset, so I get out my prayer rug and, after doing my ablutions, put my scarved head to the floor in prostration and say the prayers that I've learned.

> *Bismillaah ar-Rahman ar-Raheem*
> In the name of G-d, the infinitely Compassionate and Merciful.
> Praise be to G-d, Lord of all the worlds.
> The Compassionate, the Merciful. Ruler on the Day of Reckoning.
> You alone do we worship, and You alone do we ask for help.
> Guide us on the straight path,
> the path of those who have received your grace;
> not the path of those who have brought down wrath, nor of those who wander astray.
> Amen.

My conversion did not result from a sudden epiphany. No one had worked on me to change my religion and see the light. No one (that I remember) will get the *ajr*, or extra points in the hereafter for bringing someone born half Christian, half Jewish to the path of Islam. It was an organic evolution, a result, perhaps, of listening to the call to prayer for years and finally answering. Maybe it was the example of my Amazigh mother-in-law, who set down her prayer mat five times a day without fail and said the only prayer she knew in Arabic: the Fatiha. Or perhaps I needed to be forgiven in the language of the husband from whom I'd recently taken leave.

I'd first come to Morocco twelve years earlier. It was 1982, and I was with the Peace Corps. I had no illusion of saving the world or feeding the poor. It was just the only way I could get out of New York. Having finished a BA in literature and made progress toward a second degree in flute performance, I was itching to take leave of the city, the noise of sirens and traffic, the rats scuttling through the garbage in my East Village neighborhood, the men passed out on the Bowery, an empty bottle of wine next to their swollen faces, pee staining their pants. I wanted to escape the tired expressions staring into space on the subway. I recognized my own face in that series, as well as my father's—laborers working hard and earning little but too physically exhausted to make a change, too bound by those nets I'd been determined since childhood to avoid.

So when I saw a poster that said, "Now that you have a degree, get an education: volunteer for the Peace Corps," I took down the address and the very next day went downtown and filled out an application. I wanted to go to Gambia, enchanted as I was by the rhythms and celestial chords of the kora, a music I discovered in the Smithsonian collection of the New York Public Library. So when asked, I looked at a map of West Africa and wrote not only Gambia but all the countries that surrounded it: Guinea-Bissau, Senegal, Sierra Leone, Côte d'Ivoire, Ghana, and Mauritania.

Instead, they sent me to Morocco.

When I stepped off the plane in Casablanca in 1982, it had been six years since my summer in France, and though I had written letters to Camille all through college, I'd mostly told him about the authors I was reading—Mallarmé, Baudelaire,

Stendhal. I'd told him about my East Village apartment, my love affair with a painter, and about a seminar I was taking on French New Wave Cinema.

For his part, Camille wrote that things hadn't changed much in La Creuse, though I later learned his wife had taken her life in those years. But I was not yet his confidante. Instead, he gave me news of his grandchildren and of local and national politics (he was still the socialist mayor of the village, and hoped for a united Europe). When he learned that I was in North Africa, he was thrilled. It was, after all, the place where he had lived, the place where he'd wanted to remain, yet had left. Had his Orientalist dreams taken up residence in my subconscious during the summer we had spent together? Whatever the reason, I somehow found myself inhabiting the very region from which Camille had taken *his* leave when he was exactly my age.

For three years, I immersed myself in Moroccan culture. I lived in a mountain home with no heating in the Middle Atlas Mountains, the blood of butchered goats staining the hard mud of the weekly market where I did my shopping. I lived in a small *ryad* in the medina of Marrakech, the iron castanets of the sub-Saharan Gnawa floating over the rooftops from Jma al-Fna square during nights so hot and dry that the skin of one's heels cracked. I lived in the agricultural capital of Beni Mellal, its orange groves extending out from its perimeters and its sugar beet factories sweetening the crisp autumn air. I learned Moroccan Arabic. I perfected my French. I collected folktales and cleaned, milled, and baked the local wheat. I filled notebooks with bad poetry, threw the *I Ching* every day, and I fell in love and married a Moroccan man, bringing him "home" to Camille in France, who feted our union with the best wine from his cellar while regaling us with stories of his youth as a medical intern. My Amazigh husband and I had a baby girl, a *chileeha*, a little Berber. We spent every subsequent summer with the in-laws in Beni Mellal. I did research for my dissertation there, eventually becoming a professor at the University of Texas at Austin.

By 1994, however, my marriage had ended in divorce. My daughter was with my mother in Pennsylvania for the year, and I was in Rabat, on leave from my tenure-track job, having *taken* leave of everything but the search for a spiritual method, another way of living, of being and seeing.

How could I not embark on this path, when so many of the mystics and esoteric philosophers I had read as a student in New York had been so deeply influenced by Sufism, from Aldous Huxley to René Guénon, Frithjof Schuon and G. I. Gurdjieff? And there in Morocco the tradition was still alive. It had not (yet) been commodified like Haitian Voudun, for example, a display of the otherworldly performed on stages for foreigners. That would come soon enough with the development of spiritual tourism in Morocco. But for the time being, there was still a living tradition of Sufism, in which past and future were one. And I had a way in: I spoke Moroccan Arabic.

French too was key. One night a voice woke me from a deep sleep: "*L'homme au nord vous attend*, the man in the north is waiting for you," I heard clearly. An auditory hallucination? A message from another dimension? I had recently read a book in French on Sufism and contacted its author, the anthropologist Faouzi Skali, who would graciously receive me in his home in Fès. Soon after he introduced me to a *muqaddima*, a Sufi overseer, a woman in Casablanca who held *dhikr*, or "remembrance," ceremonies in her apartment once a week. And now there I was, hearing voices in my sleep.

How was this happening, I kept asking myself. I spoke often with a woman named Thuraya, who worked at a bank and lived in a comfortable apartment in Casablanca. She was in her forties, a widow, and her elderly mother lived with her for long stretches of time each year. Thuraya taught me how to do my ablutions, the *wudu*, and the order of the ritual washing. Most importantly, she initiated me in the Sufi order by giving me the "pact," a commitment to G-d and an acknowledgment of devotion to the shaykh (Sidi Hamza he was called, "the man in the north") as well as a series of prayers to repeat over and over, like a mantra, while sitting in meditation every day.

Meditation has always been second nature to me. I disappear easily into its embrace, whether meditating with monks in a Buddhist temple in the Bronx, which I did as a freshman in college, or in my long practice with Gurdjieff groups in the various states where I later lived. Once, while sitting in meditation in my studio in the East Village, I was stunned by a light that seemed to open behind my eyes, temporarily obliterating my body. Death before death, *fanā'* in Arabic, dissolution of the ego, annihilation in the One. For a moment, or several, I felt like the burning bush.

Islam has a language for this. It's called *al-ghayb*, absence, or *alam al-ghayb*, the invisible world. Sufis take leave of the three-dimensional realm in order to inhabit a place of visions and revelation. All the poets and mystics I'd read in college—Hildegard von Bingen, William Blake, Rudolph Steiner—had talked about this. I myself have experienced the bliss of deep contemplation throughout my life, which is probably why I

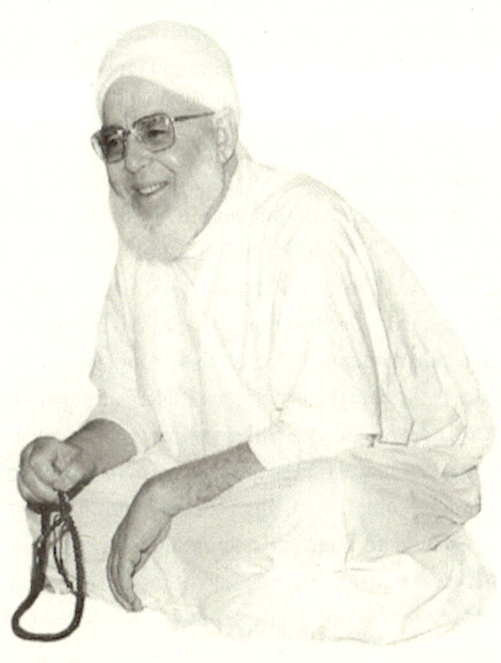

12 The shaykh of the Qadiriyya Sufi order, the largest in Morocco, Sidi Hamza (1922–2017). (Photo: Open Access)

felt an almost alchemical attraction to Sufism. I *knew* this place; it was accessed through the breath—blown into Adam in the beginning, Muslims say. But this is just a story people can understand, providing a path from the exterior (*ẓāhir*) to the interior (*bāṭin*). Sufis are not literalists; they are poets, adepts of metaphor and symbolism. It was this excavation of the soul, an articulation of a vocabulary of depth, that was drawing me in. There was something I needed to understand, something, I sensed, that I already knew but needed to remember again; *dhikr*—the Sufi ceremony of chanting the names of G-d—means "remembrance," and it is a method, a verb as well as a noun.

My memories of that year in Morocco are vivid. I am sitting in Thuraya's living room in Casablanca. The banquettes are stuffed with wool and covered with a rich gold brocade. The white carpet on the floor is thick, and prayer rugs are stacked in a pile to be unfurled at the proper time. The women are called *faqirat*, the poor ones. It is a Sufi term for a supplicant. But the women who will arrive in an hour are not poor in the least, not in the material sense. I am in a group of professional women—financiers, yoga teachers, architects—all educated in Europe and perfectly bilingual in Arabic and French. It is why the Sufi scholar in Fès sent me here, instead of introducing me to the women in Rabat where I live. I did not question it then, but now I understand: He mistook me for a member of the bourgeoisie because I am educated and an author, while I would have preferred to be with the *shaab*, the folk, the people, my class.

When the women arrive, we assemble in the living room. I join some women on the floor, while others sit on the sofa. All of us are wearing djellabas, scarves around our heads, feet in socks. A few women go into the next room to do the prayers they missed when they were at work this afternoon. One is in the bathroom doing her ablutions. When we have all returned, silence settles over us like a veil, and the ritual leader, called a *muqaddima* in Moroccan Arabic, begins chanting:

*Bismillah ar-Rahman ar-Rahim, Yā -Sīn . . .*

> In the name of G-d, the most Merciful and Compassionate, Ya-*Sīn*, by the Qur'an, full of Wisdom. You O Prophet are truly one of the messengers, upon the straight path. . . .

The Yassine Prayer is said to be the heart of the Qur'an, and these women know it by heart, though the booklets are still open in their laps, some written in Arabic, others transliterated in the Latin alphabet. I read the latter, as they are reciting too quickly for me to keep up with the Arabic script. But some of the women were brought up in French schools, and their Arabic is no more practiced than my own. Thus the transliterated booklets, for people like us, and for converts of other language groups in France and the UK. The Qur'an must be chanted in Arabic, no matter what. It is a holy text in a holy language.

We finish reciting the Yassine Surah, then we chant the Waqi'ah Surah, a chapter about the hereafter, the day of reckoning when G-d will judge the believers and those who have not believed. After that we begin to chant the names of G-d. This is the *dhikr* section, the remembrance. We start with the name Allah, the name that is pure abstraction for what is ultimately unknowable by humans, intoning the two syllables in rhythm. Al-llah, Al-llah, Al-llah, Al-llah . . . stressing the last aspirated /h/, pumping the belly all the while. It is not unlike the pranayama that I have been practicing for years, the conscious manipulation of the breath changing the brain waves until we sail into trance, taking our collective leave. But the leader brings us back enough to change the words, and we begin to chant another name, al-Latif, the Gentle or Most Subtle One. *Al-Latif, al-Latif, al-Latif, al-Latif* . . . not only is this also a name of G-d, a portal to the divine, but it is a reference to the subtle body, *aj-jism al-latif*, inhabiting each person. When the subtle body is purified—by prayer, chanting, and vigilance—the human being transforms. Sufis say such chanting "polishes the heart," and the entire being shines, emitting and attracting light. I have met people like that, people whose amplitude is turned up higher than the norm. I imagine them doing the *dhikr* continually, creating an unbroken chain to the divine even while they are speaking to others in daily life.

The more we chant, the more we become the sound. It seems to swirl us into its embrace, and yet I am aware of my body. The chanting makes my chest buzz, as it did when singing hymns in church in my youth. Polishing the heart is a good metaphor: It's at the level of the physical heart that my spirit takes leave.

Several weeks into my practice with the *faqirat* in Casablanca, Thuraya announces that Faouzi Skali will be coming to give a talk. There will be a full day of liturgy, prayer, and song, as well as a lecture by Faouzi, held at a villa somewhere in California, an elite Casablanca neighborhood. Thuraya will pick me up at the Oasis train station and we will go together.

She is there when I arrive, and I get in her small Renault wearing my djellaba, my headscarf in my bag. We take off, circling crowded roundabouts, passing buses spewing diesel fumes where children play in the street, traversing neighborhoods where thousands swelter in small apartments in the heat. Then we enter a section of town with high palm trees and bougainvillea cascading over walls that hide mansions and lawns.

Thuraya pulls over to a curb, and we get out, walking down a long private driveway full of parked cars and bordered with magnolia trees, bamboo, and eucalyptus. It is densely green, the house a stately mansion with Tudor elements—a stark contrast from the gray concrete high-rises we passed on the way over. We knock and then enter, finding ourselves in a large common area with several living rooms off to each side. Dozens of people are milling around, women—some in chic djellabas, but some in tailored suits—and men in shirts and ties. It is not sex-segregated, and most women do not have their heads covered. Although I am wearing a hand-tailored djellaba made of textured cotton, I feel like a country bumpkin.

Women place dishes on a long table a few steps above the common area. It is an open dining room that leads into the kitchen. Thuraya greets several people. And then, out of seemingly nowhere, a small dark woman with expressive eyes approaches us.

"Welcome, welcome," she says. It is Sukayna, the mistress of the house. About fifty, she is like an energetic gazelle, exuding love. She has bobbed black hair and wears slacks and a loose silk blouse. She also has a deep smoker's voice, its sultriness pleasing to me. This is a woman who cares little for convention.

"Did you see the garden?" she asks.

"Not yet."

"Come, I'll show you. We have a few minutes before lunch."

We speak in French, as do most of the people here, though it is peppered with Arabic, an upper-class code-switching.

Sukayna opens the sliding glass doors, and we walk onto the veranda. Before us is a huge expanse of perfectly manicured green grass, with flowering trees—apricot and cherry—and a section of wildflowers.

"This is magnificent," I tell her.

"It's nice," she says, smiling. She lights a cigarette and inhales deeply. "Smoke?"

I shake my head, though in fact I would like to be a partner to her sultriness.

"If you want, you can eat your lunch out here. So, you're American?"

"Yes, but my husband is Moroccan," I say. I am not quite ready to let go of that narrative, although the divorce proceedings have begun.

"Where is he from?"

"The north, he's Beni Iznassen."

"So is the shaykh, you know. That's not a coincidence."

She squints her eyes and looks into mine.

I knew that Yahya, my daughter's father, was from the same tribe or *qabila* as the shaykh of the order. I had married into holy lineage years before. Was that what I had felt when I first met my future father-in-law? I remember knowing right there and then that I would have Yahya's child.

"Let's go in," she says. "It's time to eat. I'm glad you're with us."

People have already started queuing for lunch, taking a plate from one end of the table and filling it as they proceed to the other. Fish tagine with olives, lamb tagine with prunes, tomato-and-pepper salad, aubergine, and grated carrot with orange juice. Warm bread is in a basket. The offerings are copious.

"Get yourself some food," Sukayna says to me. "I'll see you later."

I serve myself, then head back to the garden, where I speak with a university student studying to be a doctor. I speak with the wife of a diplomat as well as a French expat who has been living in Casablanca for more than forty years with her Moroccan husband. The future minister of religion is also here, though I don't meet him that day.

When we finish eating, we bring our plates to the kitchen and move into the living room, leaving our shoes outside the door, settling on the banquettes and on the thick carpeted floor, men and women together, unveiled and unbothered. When everyone has settled, Faouzi Skali begins to speak.

*A'udhu billahi min ash-Shaytan ar-rajim, bismillah ar-Rahman ar-Rahim*, he begins in Arabic. "I seek refuge in G-d from the outcast Satan, in the name of G-d, the most merciful and compassionate. . . ."

But then he quickly turns to French.

"There is a dark tunnel in the infinite light," he says. "We call that time. When a human enters this tunnel, we call that birth, *n'est-ce pas*? Don't we?"

He looks up. We are all hanging on his words.

"We walk through this tunnel during our lifetime. Until we come out on the other end: death."

Faouzi pauses, smiling. He seems to be looking at something in another dimension.

"We imagine that life is an evolution in this trajectory of time. That, I would say, is an illusion. Science pierces holes in the tunnel, letting in some light. When we remember that there is light *outside* the tunnel, we call that faith. But when we see the light *in* the dark, that, that is love. And when we see the light *through* the tunnel, despite its obscurity, that is wisdom."

A man in the room gives an affirmation: "*Allah, Allah*," he says aloud.

"We can illuminate the tunnel with our own light. Those who can do that are saints. But when the tunnel and the light become one," Faouzi continues, "there are no words for that state."

He pauses. My eyes are focused on his, which are large and hypnotic. He seems like he is already floating somewhere outside the tunnel. And for the first time since childhood, I see an aura. Blue and luminous, it surrounds him.

Faouzi speaks some more. People ask questions. Some are about the relation of Sufism to Islam. The *dhikr*, he says, only comes *after* all the other obligations—prayer, charity, fasting. It does not replace them. He also mentions an upcoming music festival in Fès. The whirling dervishes will perform, as well as gospel singers from the United States and of course Sufi sung poetry of several Moroccan brotherhoods. There is going to be a conference as well, with some of the brightest minds in interfaith dialogue—Christians, Buddhists, Muslims, as well as neuroscientists from the Max Planck Institute. Faouzi asks us to volunteer, to be ushers and to do other organizational chores. This will be the first of many decades of the Fès Festival of World Sacred Music, an event that even the Dalai Lama will imitate.

Faouzi suggests we break into groups to do the liturgy. The women get up, and I follow them into another room. The men stay with him. Booklets are passed out. Women grab their scarves and cover their heads. We begin, as always, with the Yassine Surah, and proceed to the *dhikr*. When the liturgy ends and the singing starts, the woman next to me swoons, her eyes rolling back in her head, her body swaying. We are all taken up, clapping our hands and smiling from ear to ear. It is a bit like the Christian revival meetings I experienced as a teenager, and just as I did at that time, I feel like an outsider, embarrassed at the zeal with which these women let go into adulation of the shaykh.

At the end of the evening, with the light outside fading, we are served tea and sweets—marzipan gazelle horns and sesame cookies—and then slowly everyone leaves, thanking Sukayna as they file out the door.

"I'll see you soon," she says to me. "Thuraya, give Nedjma my number."

Nedjma is my name in Morocco. (*Deborah* sounds too much like *debr-ras-ak*, "mind your own business.") Nedjma means "star" in Arabic. I like the sound of the /d/ and the /j/ together, like fudge, even though that pronunciation is more Algerian than Moroccan. It is an old name, one not used anymore, much like Gertrude or Hazel in the United States. It is also the name of my Jewish grandmother: Stella, like the stars to which G-d gave each a name (Psalm 147:4), like Abraham's descendants who will be as numerous as stars in the sky (Genesis 15:5).

I continued to attend liturgies for the better part of a year, commuting back and forth from Rabat to Casablanca. I studied the Sufi philosophers I could find in English and French. Al-Ghazali, who says that music is a path to gnosis. Ibn al-Arabi, for whom all of existence rests on the paradox of "He is and He isn't" (*Huwa/laysa Huwa*). There is nothing but an undelimited and unknowable G-d (*Huwa*), he says. And yet an infinity of delimited forms also exist (*laysa Huwa*), all of them with names and attributes. It's as if G-d were dreaming a dream; the characters and circumstances are endlessly various, but without the dreamer, they all disappear. And yet the dream, too, is real. It is not an illusion, just a different density of vibration, a part of a larger whole.

I'd end up spending many sleepless nights singing at the shaykh's sanctuary near the Moroccan border with Algeria. I'd watch as women, with eyes closed, threw their heads forward onto their chests and back into the air, their hair loosening from their scarves, as their bare feet pounded the floor in time to the singing of praises on the *Mawlid*, the Prophet's birthday. But this is not the only leave-taking I'd witness. I would also experience my own departure from the quotidian into other states, not only attending Sufi rituals but participating in spirit possession ceremonies in Rabat as well. I began trafficking with the jinn, taking leave of my senses in multiple ways.

How did I move from the relative conservatism of a Sufi ceremony to the Dionysian abandon of a possession cult, an activity that some consider devil worship? For unlike the Qadiriyya Sufis, who have a hagiography that extends back through the centuries to Iran, the Gnawa came up from sub-Saharan Africa. Their culture is oral, their text is the body. They propitiate the spirits with music that induces trance, burning incense appropriate to each spirit and throwing veils of different colors over those possessed. They cut themselves with knives and hold bundles of burning candles under their chins and forearms, not flinching in the least.

Some say the spirits afflict you when you are most open and vulnerable. Yes, I had read a book by anthropologist Vincent Crapanzano in which I learned about the trance and mortification rituals of the Hamadsha, another Moroccan possession cult. But mine was not an intellectual interest. It was the music of the Gnawa that drew me in, the same music I'd heard over and over since coming to Morocco in 1982, a sub-Saharan beat played on the bass-sounding *hajhuj* and accompanied by large metal castanets. It was the music and, I think now, the fact that I myself needed to placate the anxious spirits whose whispers I'd heard throughout my life without knowing from where they were emanating. I had taken leave of my marriage and, for that year, of my daughter as well. I had taken leave of the institution that employed me, of my language and my country. I had entered another reality, one in which I'd begun to hear music without a source, smell incense where none was burning, hear voices, and also have visions.

I had heard about the reputation of the brilliant scholar Abdelhai Diouri, who had studied with my hero Roland Barthes and was Morocco's leading authority on all of its trance cults. I decided to contact him and, after a few conversations to discern my sincerity and my psychological strength, Diouri took me to see the main Gnawa master, or *maalim*, in Rabat; Gnawa, from the word *Guinea* perhaps, or from the Amazigh word *aguinaw*, meaning "black man." The Gnawa ceremonies combine sub-Saharan African rituals and music with North African beliefs. It is a syncretic tradition, much like Candomblé or Santeria in Central and South America; in this case, a mix of Moroccan Islam and Voudun brought by West African captives mostly in the fifteenth and sixteenth centuries.

Si Mohammed was bone thin and very dark complected, missing two front teeth and living in a shantytown of cinder block homes in the neighborhood of Youssefia. His grandmother, he told me over tea, grew up as a slave, *aabida* (fem.), in the royal palace and was a *muqaddima*, or overseer of possession rituals—the king's personal clairvoyant. There is a pantheon, I learn, that stretches from Tangier to Timbuktu and beyond, to Mauritania, Sierra Leone, Guinea, and Ghana. It stretches east to Algeria and as far as Egypt, though with other names. Si Mohammed agreed to have me attend the *lilas*, or "nights" of divination and propitiation for the possessed and their possessors.

When I go to my first *lila* I am immediately swept away. The music makes my chest vibrate, and my body is taken up in the beat. I am in a family home deep in the medina of Rabat, with an inner courtyard. The musicians arrive as if in parade, hitting their snare drums to alert the guests, the neighbors, and, most importantly, the spirits that they are arriving. Candles are lit, offerings in place. A goat has been sacrificed in preparation for the ceremony.

Once inside, the Gnawa warm up the crowd with music and dances *not* meant to invoke the spirits. This is the *laaba*, the play, the opening of the gates to the more serious work that awaits. We will be at it all night, the sung invocations to the spirits, each with their accompanying colors, incense, and foods to be ingested: the anise bread, raisin water, milk infused with sugar, rose petals, and orange blossoms, a kind of communion. Musk, black and white benzoin, ambergris, frankincense, sandalwood, and myrrh will be put on the brazier and the smoke wafted in the faces of those present. This is enough to make some women get up and trance, thrusting their thoraxes forward, their buttocks back, their heads swinging side to side like a pendulum in time to the castanets. Trance. Transcendence. Transformation. Transmigration. And even transgender, as women are possessed by male spirits, and men with those of women.

One night I find myself in a small ground floor apartment in the Océan neighborhood of Rabat. There is a small exterior where the Gnawa begin the ceremony, beating their snare drums while wafting incense in the direction of a woman covered in a white veil. Once inside, the ceremony begins in earnest, and I watch a man get up to trance to the beat of his possessing jinn, Sidi Hamou, the god of the slaughterhouse, reputed to be the "hardest" and most demanding of all the jinn, with the exception perhaps of Aisha Qandisha, the temptress, a chimera with cloven feet.

The room is small, lit only with a bulb that hangs from the ceiling. Mbaraka, the *muqaddima*, attends to a woman who is on her knees, prostrate before the musicians, breathing heavily and moaning. The rest of us sit on sagging banquettes covered in worn red floral fabric. I am just an observer here. All eyes and ears, my body as if elsewhere, my own subjectivity absent.

Suddenly a man gets up to trance. He is about forty, wearing jeans and a T-shirt. He raises his arms high in the air, his head bowed, then brings his arms down and scissors them back and forth in front of his knees. I'll come to understand this gesture as an acknowledgment of the four directions of the winds, *riyah*, also the word for spirits. It is a sign of the crossroads, the crossing over from the quotidian to the spiritual, the unmappable place of in-between.

He sets his intention. I can see it in his eyes, which are somehow otherworldly now. He is absent, and yet he is present. He reaches down to a copper tray near his sandaled feet and picks up a small tea glass. He empties the sugary remains into his mouth and then proceeds to put the glass itself between his jaws. I hear it crack between his teeth and imagine it cutting his soft palate, though no blood appears. I watch as he chews with concentration, the larger pieces becoming smaller, the sound of glass crunching against tooth enamel. We are all focused on this terrible feat, like a crowd watching a bullfight. The castanets have fallen silent, but the *hajhuj* continues its baseline beat. It is a holy moment of sorts. And then he swallows—he has ingested it all. Nothing remains of the glass, but he remains standing, swaying his body. He moans and falls to the floor but then is helped to his place on the banquette. No one seems to be alarmed. The *muqaddima* has clearly seen this before. For her, the night will unfold as it usually does: Different jinn will be appeased, other people will trance, taking sharp knives to their skin, squeezing their necks with scarves until they fall gasping to their knees, their faces paled to a bluish-white.

I'd get used to walking home to my comfortable apartment just after dawn, the weak light breaking over the silent city, before the diesel-spewing buses began running and the streets filled with people. I'd float home like a spirit above the cracked sidewalks, the cafés still empty, the smell of baking croissants in the salty seaside air, these walks that let me somehow integrate what I'd witnessed. How is it that people transcend their bodies this way, without seeming to suffer? How is it that self-inflicted pain becomes itself a salve? Was anything healing within *me*? Or was I myself falling prey to a subtle but seductive net?

I needed to know, and after a few months of observation at several other ceremonies, I, too, take the floor. I can't resist. My mother was a dancer after all. I grew up doing turns and spins, splits, back bends, and pliés in our living room. I could turn around and around like a dervish without getting dizzy, having learned how to spot, how to find my center like a top on its axis. I understood intuitively that movement relied on stasis and could balance the two from an early age. And so, I take leave of everything except this sensation and give myself over to the dance. I look at it that way at first, observing the trancers like a choreographer studies movement. But I soon understand that this movement is in service to a state of being, and in such states, rapture ensues. It leaves a golden sweat on one's brow; an aura of bliss infuses one's bones and the room.

In trance, I am transported, the edges of my skin melding with the incensed air, the gut strings of the *hajhuj* becoming my sinews and limbs, the taste of the music, my food. The *qraqab*, those heavy metal castanets, are my heartbeat and my flesh a pulsing cell in a body much larger than my own. There is, in fact, no *me*, no *us*, but something else. *It* moves me, *it* moves within me—its thoughts, its impulses. And yet I never lose consciousness. I observe as I trance, and the memories of this state, what is called *al-hal* in Arabic, imprint my psyche with a map of an eternal dance. I taste this and become a devotee in what, in another era, might be called a cult of Dionysus. And yet my volition remains intact. The author in me is never absent.

Not all the trancers are euphoric, however. There are those whose movements are more epileptic than anything else. And I wonder if indeed they have that malady, falling on the floor with jerking limbs, their lips trembling, their eyes rolled back in their heads. These women are *maskun*, "inhabited" by Sidi Mimoun, or Sidi Abdelqadr, by Lalla Mira or Lalla Malika. But who is to say what really possesses them, a spirit, a syndrome, a trauma, a disease? I leave those questions of belief aside. For me, in my body, there is something taking leave, and something else that resides: ecstasy.

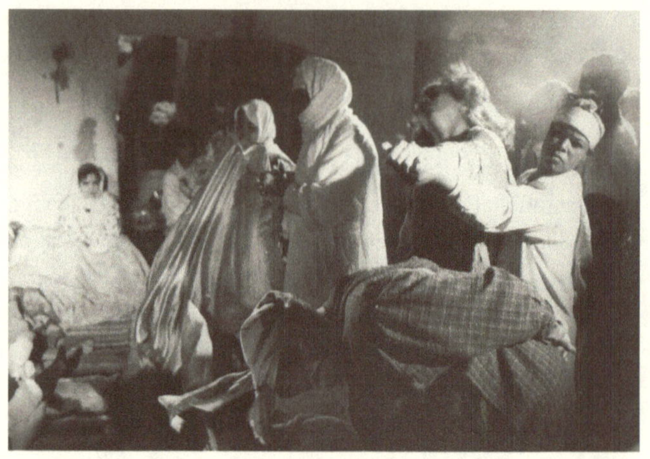

**13** Entranced. Possessed women at a Gnawa ceremony. (Photo: Ariane Smolderen)

A year passes in this way, in ongoing swings between devotion and delirium, between absence and presence, between the Sufi sacred and the Gnawa profane, between Casablanca and Rabat. I am living in the *barzakh*, literally the "in-between," the realm in Sufi cosmology where material things are spiritualized and spiritual realities take shape, a place of visions and dreams.

At the Sufi liturgies we'd pray and sit quietly until someone experienced the *hal*, the state, an unbidden inspiration, not unlike being filled with the spirit in Christianity, resulting in spontaneous exclamations of "Allah!" Both Sufi disciples and those possessed by spirits share a gestural vocabulary: stamping the floor, arms raised, head and eyes tilted back in rapture. But while the body movements are similar, the intention is different. Sufis praise G-d and the Prophet /pbuh/ while the Gnawa propitiate the spirits that live in the realm between heaven and earth, in the world of magic and power. There are many in-betweens, an infinity really. For Ibn al-Arabi, there are nothing *but* in-betweens, stations between stations between stations, where one is forever taking leave for somewhere else.

One day I told Thuraya, the Sufi *muqaddima*, that I was doing research on the Gnawa. I called it research to distinguish it from my practice with the Sufi order, but in fact I'd become infatuated with the music, the incense, the movement, the rapture. *Al-bliya* is what the Gnawa call it—addiction. It is commonly acknowledged: once you've lived in the beat, you want more. I begin to hear it even when I am far from its source. Is it coming from under someone's door? Is there a ceremony down the hall? But no, it is in my body, it inhabits me. I am possessed by what it *does* to me.

"It's a good thing you're in the tariqa," Thuraya said, referring to the Sufi order. "The Gnawa are dangerous, but the shaykh will protect you."

She was talking about the pact, the vows I took swearing my devotion to the shaykh, the man in the north who, said that voice in my dreams, was waiting for me. There is no leaving this contract. Of course, one can be a "bad Muslim." I am. But the shaykh, like G-d, is forgiving and compassionate. Once in the tariqa, always in the tariqa. Once initiated into the secret, one can never forget it. Or if one does, woe to that person, for awakening and then falling asleep again is no one's fault but one's own.

The secret. It's what, in the end, I'd gone to Morocco to discover. The Sufis speak of it often: *as-sirr*. It's what the shaykh has, and what the disciple seeks. It is not in books. You won't read it here. It's in the gaze of the shaykh, in the taste of the *dhikr*, in the love that circulates from heart to heart when doing the work of worship, and the way that life unfolds with remarkable synchronicity thereafter. Like a spirit, the secret also inhabits, residing in the flesh like a seeded genetic code, that remains unexpressed if forgotten. Thus the practice of *dhikr*, remembrance. It's about orientation. The qibla, the direction you face when praying, is just a symbol for this turning toward, a taking leave of one state to better enter the next.

Can the person in the dream become aware of the dreamer and yet simultaneously inhabit their separateness? Can the dreamer and the dreamed become consciously one? This is presence, says Ibn al-Arabi, the paradox of unity and diversity in one breath. Call it G-d. Call it Atman. Call it light or the subatomic realm. But call upon it often, say the Sufis, as life changes when one does.

One night I awake with another voice in my ear. *Hnaya n-sabaqu*, the voice says in Moroccan Arabic, "we will win out." I open my eyes and to my right is a head, just a head, with bulbous eyes and jowls. And somehow, I know that this is Sidi Mimoun, the spirit of the forest, the West African spirit who can morph into a lion, the one to whose music I first tranced. My heart is beating fast, and I am paralyzed with fright. And then the head disappears, and I reach for the light.

Most would think this an imaginary emanation, a mere phantasm. And indeed, I explain it to myself and others by saying I had so immersed myself in the world of the Gnawa that their images and archetypes came to inhabit me, manifesting in dreams that pierced the veil of sleep. But it may also be that the

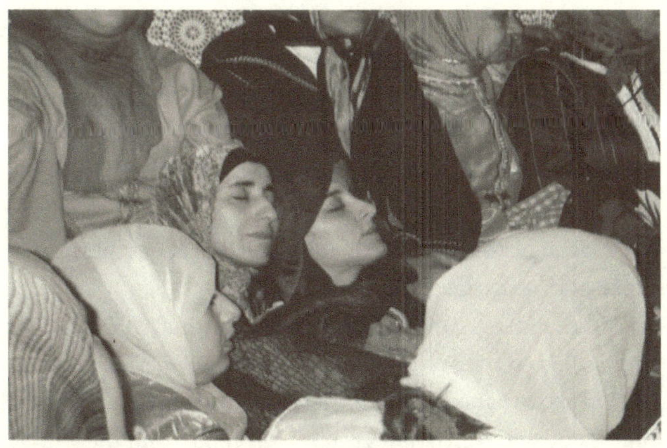

14 Sufi women in ecstatic rapture at the Sufi sanctuary in northern Morocco. (Photo: Deborah Kapchan)

curtain that usually keeps the visible and the invisible realms separate has parted. For a moment, or several, I have infrared vision. For what else is possession if not a state resulting from an opening, a disclosure of one world in another? But also a tear in the fabric of misrecognition that keeps humans gently asleep in our dreams, the ones wherein we mistake what we can see for all that is.

It's the morning of my second excursion in old Jerusalem, and I wake extra early to meet Adam, a Christian guide, just outside the Jaffa Gate. He immediately drives me to the Mount of Olives in his car and parks just above the Jewish cemetery. From there, in the cool of the morning and in the company of several white-speckled bulbul, he points out the original perimeter of Jerusalem that once extended outside its current walls to what is now called the City of David. He also shows me where the palace of Pontius Pilate is thought to have been, the place where Jesus was condemned, as well as the prison where he was then taken to begin his walk with the cross. It's as if we are looking at a map of history on the adjoining hill, the geographical distance mirroring the distance back in time.

Now I understand why Adam insisted we meet so early. The tourists haven't arrived yet, and we are alone with our contemplation of this panorama of stories. Even though he is a popular tour guide with Christian groups that come from the United States, I can tell from our moments of shared silence that he, too, is moved. While we gaze across a sea of Jewish headstones sloping down toward the Golden Gate and the Dome of the Rock, I broach the subject of the Trinity.

"I was brought up Protestant," I begin, "and was taught that the Father, the Son and the Holy Spirit are *symbolically* one, but that Jesus himself was a man, the son of G-d, yes, but divine in the way that *all* humans are: through the Holy Spirit, the eternal in us." I tell him that I learned that Jesus was a representative of G-d on earth, but not G-d himself. "We distinguished ourselves from the Catholics that way," I explain.

"No," he corrects me, without missing a beat. "For Protestants, Jesus *is* the incarnate G-d, not a man."

"For all Protestants?" I ask. "Maybe my interpretation is Presbyterian or Methodist. I attended both those churches in my youth. Or maybe this is just what my mother believed, that we all have the Holy Spirit and so are all sons and daughters of G-d and that Jesus showed the way to that realization."

"Jesus *was* the way," Adam insists, "and the Truth and the Life. I'm an Evangelical. For us, Jesus is G-d. There is no distinction. 'I and my father are one,' he told his disciples."

"I spent time in an Evangelical church when I was an adolescent," I confess. It is a phase in my life I'm usually too embarrassed to discuss, but with Adam the way is paved. "We studied the Bible," I venture, "and spoke in tongues." I remember it being like saying prayers while taking leave of all meaning.

He nods, as if this is the most natural thing in the world. I feel he doesn't want to go further with this conversation, but I am paying him dearly for half a day's work. I want to understand his perspective.

Thinking back on the Christian phase of my youth now, I see it was just as much a means to get away from the blaring noise of the television in our small suburban apartment as anything else, an escape from the alcoholic rages of my stepfather Tom that sent us searching for motels in the middle of the night. Is alcoholism so different from spirit possession? My stepfather became someone else, a jinn like Sidi Hamou, who exacted sacrifice. With every drink, he took leave of the little boy with flames encircling his body writhing in pain and calling for help, and became himself the flames that burned everyone else. In contrast to my tumultuous homelife, however, the prayer meetings were calm, held at the home of a young woman in my high school who lived in a mansion. We used to sit in one of the dens on the second floor, our Bibles open in our laps, and read different verses out loud, marking the mar-

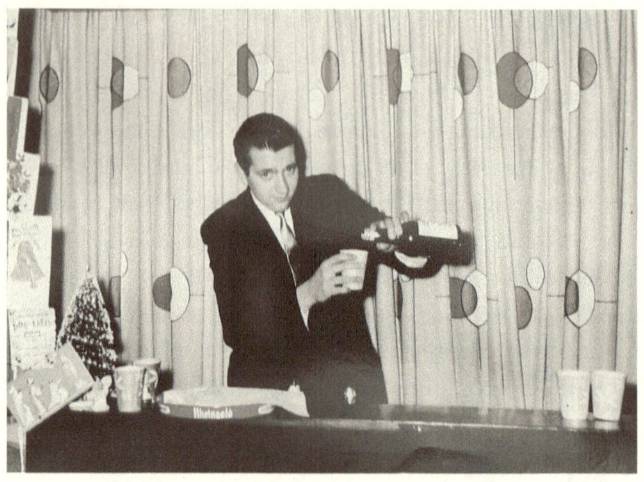

**15** Thomas Venute (TV Tom), circa 1959, at the Christmas party at the Arthur Murray Dance Studios in the Bronx. (Photo: Author's Family Archives)

gins with fine architectural pens: predictions of the arrival of the Messiah in Isaiah, praises for the merciful G-d in Psalms, stories of Jesus, his Sermon on the Mount, with promises of abundant blessings and eternal life.

"I am the path, the truth and the life," Adam quoted.

Just this simple sentence contained so many meanings, and my high school friends and I discussed them together: the "I am" in Exodus when G-d in the form of a burning bush tells Moses, "I am that I am." The "I am" that is Christ, a self-evidence, an assertion of Being, a verb made a noun, a divinity made flesh. And then the path, the truth, the life—a map for taking one's leave.

At the monthly regional meetings of this Christian group, we also spoke in tongues. It was easy to have phonemes come out of my mouth, to string them together in what linguist Roman Jakobson might call "tongue delirium," a return to the stage even prior to the imitative babble of babyhood. Humans speak many languages. Might there not be more of them, ones that existed somewhere deep in the recesses of the human unconscious? Is that not the purity of song?

We head toward Adam's car again, and as we walk, I ask him about his life and family. He tells me that he came to Jerusalem after college in his early twenties and married a Jewish convert to Christianity. They're bringing up their four children as Christians and live in a community with other families of similar belief.

"If you don't mind me asking," I say, "how do your wife's parents feel about that?"

"She was brought up Orthodox, an Orthodox Jew," he clarifies, "but as a teenager she had an American boyfriend who was Evangelical, her first relationship. He brought her to Christ. It didn't work out with him, and he went back to the United States, but then she met me. By that time, she was a practicing Christian."

"And so her parents have accepted her conversion?"

"More or less." He looks at me with half a smile. "There are a lot of Messianic Jews in Israel."

I wonder about this, about the numbers. Just yesterday I asked Avi why there was tension between the Christians and the Jews, something less palpable in the United States.

"All the violence against Jews has taken place in Christian lands," he answered immediately. "Think about it: the Crusades, the pogroms, the Holocaust. These all arose in Christendom."

Christendom. It's a word I equate with the Middle Ages (and with Monty Python movies as well). But he had a point. And here in this city of Jerusalem where history is so palpable, it is hard to forget. What's more, the economy depends on differences remaining differences. Markets and shrines have always existed side by side, and pilgrimage is big business. But even money—or perhaps especially money—relies on a narrative. People travel the world to consume stories. And Jerusalem churns them out. It is a storytelling industry. And that is why I am here: to gather them. But aren't I also waiting for something to move in me, to tell me which story to enter definitively, so to take my leave of the other two?

The tourists are starting to arrive, and we head toward the car and drive down the hill to Gethsemane and the church that has been built next to the walled garden. We stand and gaze at the ancient olive trees, hollowed by time, some living branches still growing from their desiccated trunks. I marvel at these old beings, so wide around it would take three or four people to circle their girth, if, of course, people were allowed to get close.

"Are these trees really more than two thousand years old?" I ask Adam.

"Unlikely," he says, "but they are hundreds of years old."

Still, not the ones under which the disciples slept the night Jesus was betrayed by Judas. Not the ones under which he prayed, wakeful, before the fateful march to the Crucifixion. And yet, their craggy bark and knotted arthritic branches, the humus that holds their roots strong to the earth, gives me pause. I listen to what they have to tell me. And though I am not able to translate their message into words, I understand, through my very breath, what they are saying. This is the way

Jerusalem communicates—through the stories in the earth that come up through one's bones and enter one's cells like a quantum of ghosts.

Yesterday with Avi we passed policemen and women shaking down some Arabs in the street outside the Austrian Hospice.

"They're from the territories," Avi said, when he saw me staring.

"How can you tell?"

"By the way they dress—their T-shirts and jeans."

I watched, horrified at this performance of stop-and-frisk, and noticed more police, this time behind barricades to our right.

"That's so they can't be charged or killed in the crowd," he told me.

I think of the three Jews that had just been stabbed near the Jaffa Gate.

Adam and I reach the car, then drive down the hill and up the adjoining slope to park near the Lion's Gate, what Christians call Saint Stephen's Gate. It is the beginning of the Via Dolorosa, he explains, the stations of the cross. Before we set out on the path, however, we stop at Saint Anne's church. Like so many monuments in Jerusalem, the archaeological history of this site encompasses many centuries and belief systems. The church stands on what was once a pagan shrine to the god of healing (Asclepius). A Byzantine basilica was built over those remains in the fifth century, and then, in the 1130s, the Crusaders built a church renowned for its acoustics on the very same site, named after the mother of Mary, because it is also thought to be atop the grotto where Mary, "the mother of G-d," grew up.

Adam says that pilgrims come to this church to sing, to experience its acoustical wonders, the swirl of sound disintegrating the boundaries between the body's flesh and the flesh of the world. We peek in, but a Christian tour group from Italy is listening to their guide explain its history, so we continue walking about a hundred meters farther to the pool of Bethesda. Here we put our elbows on a barrier and gaze down at excavated walls and steep stone stairs leading to a basin of water far below.

"This is one of the most accurate archaeological sites in the city," Adam explains. "We are almost sure that this is where Christ healed the lame man on the Sabbath."

Adam went on to retell that story: how Christ told the paralyzed man to get up, and the man did, and yet that very act of healing brought criticism to Jesus because he was performing miracles on the Sabbath, the day of rest.

"So, this was both a miracle and a defiance of Jewish law," I say.

"Exactly. Jesus wasn't interested in following any laws but two: Love G-d and love one's neighbor as oneself."

"'On that hang all the laws of the prophets,'" I offer, recalling my days as a student of the Gospels.

But Adam knows that one by heart.

"Yes, Matthew 22," he says. "'And Jesus said unto him, Thou shalt love the Lord thy G-d with all thy heart, and with all thy soul, and with all thy mind. This is the first and great commandment. And the second is like unto it, Thou shalt love thy neighbor as thyself. On these two commandments hang all the law *and* the prophets.'"

"Sounds simple," I remark, noticing where I had misquoted. "But loving one's neighbor in Jerusalem is not easy these days."

"It has never been easy," says Adam. "Jesus knew Jewish law by heart. He was extremely learned. He came to replace those laws with love." But love is a very high station. Not many achieve it.

I look over the wall that protects the site and imagine the paretic man being carried down those stairs to touch the water, to be healed by Christ. Was it an act of faith on the man's part, or of desperation? Or are those somehow the same? Where is that healing power today? Where is faith? My own has flown away, taken leave on wings of imaginary angels.

The sound of chanting interrupts our contemplation, and we return to the church, where the pilgrims are now singing their praises. We stand at the narthex, the threshold of inside and out, as their voices hit our sternums, vaulting us upward.

The rest of the morning is spent walking through the old city. We see a group of Christian pilgrims from the Philippines, one carrying a large cross on his shoulder.

"You can rent those crosses," Adam tells me, as we pass, "for about fifteen dollars a day."

At each station, a crowd of pilgrims gathers. Adam has done this many times, and in fact I passed this way just yesterday with Avi, so we do not tarry, but Adam brings things to my attention as we make our way through the crowds.

"This is where he stumbled," Adam says, and later on, "This is where Simon helped him carry the cross."

We pass a small neighborhood mosque.

"Only Muslims can enter," he says. "But look."

He stops. A large banner printed with a verse from the Qur'an hangs just inside the open door for all to see: "Say: He is G-d, the One and Only. G-d, the Eternal, Absolute. He begetteth not, nor is He begotten. And there is none like unto Him."

"That's the prayer that refutes Christ in Islam," Adam says to me. "You'll notice it's printed in English."

I had said that prayer many times with the Sufis, but never had thought of it that way. Yet now I see the critique in those words, especially when they're put on display. Muslims, like Jews, maintain G-d as an unknowable mystery, whereas for Christians "he" becomes a flesh-and-blood mortal, an individual, a being who experiences death and, in the end, overcomes it, at least according to the story. No wonder Christianity was considered revolutionary. It broke with the reigning paradigm, catapulting the human imagination into an entirely new form of subjectivity.

The *via negativa*, the negative path, also exists in Christianity however, the path that leads only to the cloud of unknowing, a nonplace wherein humans submit to the impossibility of understanding—the state wherein all attempts to delimit divinity fail, because unlike words that circumscribe meaning, G-d is limitless, unable to be defined. In the cloud of unknowing, one lingers in the discomfort of paradox, of being and nonbeing, until something shifts, an opening appears, and the seeker is elsewhere, perplexed but also in awe. Sufis, like the Gnawa, call this *al-hal*, the state. For Jews it is a glimpse of the Ein Sof, the endless—what is beyond attribute and human understanding.

We end at the Church of the Holy Sepulchre, the house of worship built on top of what is thought to be Calvary, the place of the Crucifixion and the site of Jesus's tomb as well. Pilgrims are kissing a flat stone on the floor near the entrance.

"That's the slab where the body of Christ is thought to have been washed after his death," Adam explains. "It's probably no more than a century or two old." I reach down and touch it nonetheless.

"So, none of this is from Jesus's time?" I ask, as I stand up again.

"Very little," he says. "These mosaics here are from the twentieth century. You see what's under the ground at the feet of Jesus on the cross?" He points to the image on the wall before us.

"A skull."

"It's Adam's skull. The story says that Jesus was crucified on the very site of Adam's grave, and that Jesus's blood reached down to redeem all of humanity, beginning with Adam's original sin."

The crowds are thickening. It is hot, and in any case, I was here yesterday, so we leave the church and walk to the site of the upper room. People are standing in line to enter, and someone is impatiently telling the person ahead to move on.

"Is this really the place of the Last Supper?" I ask, incredulous.

"Probably not," Adam admits. "The upper room is just a term for the place where one receives guests. There are several references to the upper room in the Bible. Most likely they are not all the same one. But the Last Supper was supposed to have taken place near the Tomb of David, which is right around the corner."

We go there next. Here the entrances are divided by gender.

"I'll meet you outside," Adam says.

A strikingly beautiful Orthodox Jewish woman sits by the door, dressed in white and wearing a large turban on her head.

She is reading the Torah. Further in, there is a tomb covered in green velvet before which a nun and some others are seated, each reading their own version of the Holy Book. It is an ecumenical site of worship.

"What's in that tomb?" I ask Adam when I find him on the street.

"There's nothing in any of these tombs," he says blithely. "A body doesn't last for thousands of years."

"It's a place marker then?"

He nods. "Something like that."

We end the morning by visiting a tomb of someone supposed never to have died at all—Mary, the "mother of G-d," at the Dormitio Sanctae Mariae, the Church of the Holy Sleeping Mary. For Catholics, Mary had no sin and thus did not, could not, die, but rather was assumed into heaven already transformed, as all Christians will be at the return of Christ.

The church itself is packed when we go in, so we make a quick left and go down the spiral staircase to the crypt, but not before I quickly cross myself, for the formality. Downstairs we are alone. The figure of sleeping Mary reclines on top of a tomb, her robe carved in cherrywood, her face and praying hands in white ivory. Fresh white lilies surround her, and there are radiant mosaics depicting the life of Christ in each alcove in the vaulted room.

But then I notice that we are not quite alone. There is a young couple seated behind a wooden barrier under a mosaic portraying Jesus and his disciples. The woman is seated cross-legged on a mat facing the image but also facing the man, who sits directly under the figure of Jesus, his long hair, like that in the image, falling on his shoulders.

Adam has gone upstairs, but I linger and hesitantly return to the couple, who seem to be having a holy moment. The man smiles at me beatifically, puts his hands in the position of prayer and bows his head in assent. It seems he thinks I'm going to take his picture and while I would like to do so, I don't, but instead point my camera above their heads at the mosaic.

"Did you see the couple in the crypt?" I ask Adam when I join him outside.

"The Jerusalem syndrome," he says. "People come here and start believing they are prophets. Funny thing is that I heard them speaking Hebrew."

Messianic Jews, I think. Like Adam's wife? But that's different, isn't it? How to draw the line between delusion and belief? Isn't all conversion a taking leave, even if into the imagination? But some imaginations are shared, and some are not. Still, collective hysteria also exists. It surrounds us in Jerusalem and elsewhere. Imaginations materialize in sometimes horrifying ways. When does the dark string of night appear as the light string of day?

When I stood on my first day, head covered, at the Western Wall with the Jewish pilgrims, I prayed for the memory of my Jewish father and my recently deceased mother, born and raised a Christian, but submerged in a mikvah by her mother-in-law's decree, converting to Judaism to marry my father. I prayed for my children, for their lives and their safety, as I prayed for my own. I did not pray for peace among nations, did not pray for the Jewish people, the chosen, nor for the Christian church. I did not pray for the *ummah*, the Muslim believers, though

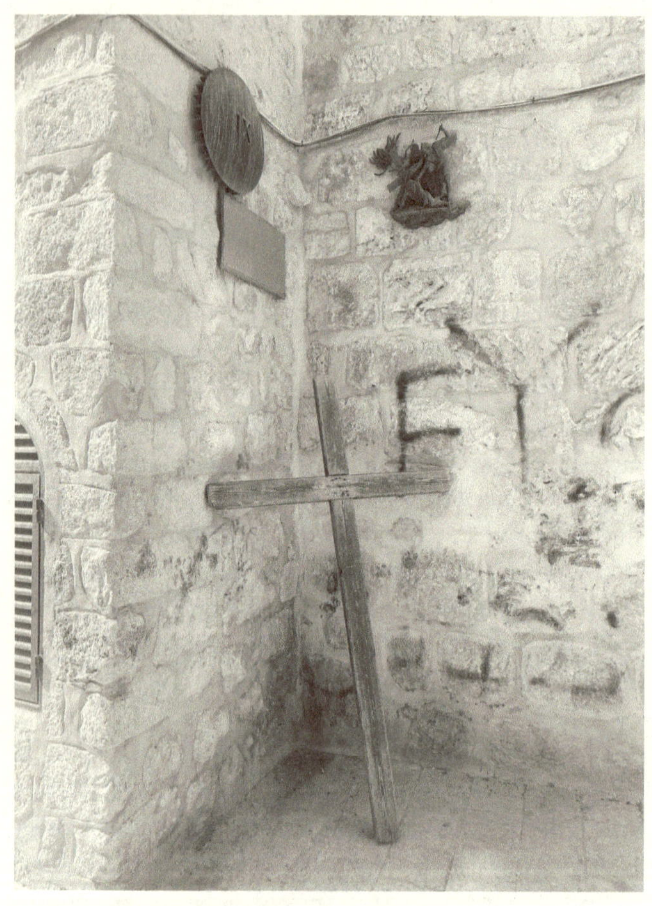

**16** A rental cross for Christian pilgrims in Jerusalem at one of the stations of the cross. (Photo: Deborah Kapchan)

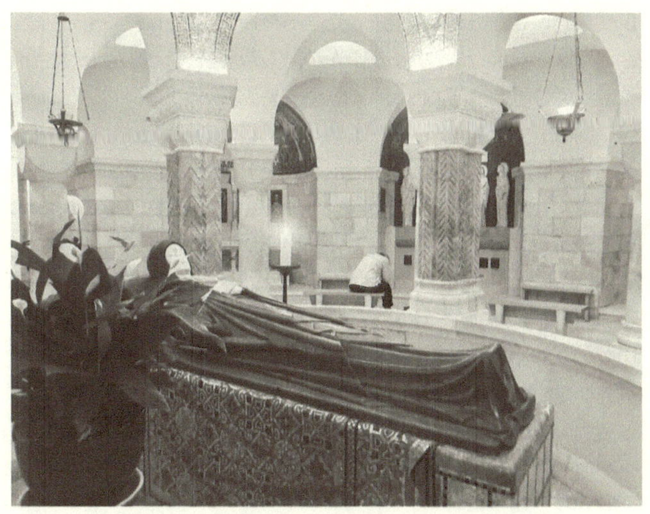

17 “Sleeping Mary” on the tomb of Mary at the Church of Dormition in Jerusalem where she supposedly fell asleep until the second coming. (Photo: Deborah Kapchan)

I had stood in synagogues, churches, and mosques while listening to clerics exhort G-d in “his” mercy and compassion to pour blessings on each of these separate communities. I did not even pray for the People of the Book (ahl al-kitāb, أهل الكتاب), an Arabic term referring to the three monotheistic religions. Rather, I prayed for the two parents I had now lost, making me now both an orphan and the elder in my small family of two children. Selfish prayers, self-sustaining, for without my children I could not go on living on earth.

Today, my final day in Jerusalem, I will go to the Dome of the Rock, the place where Muslims believe Abraham was asked by G-d to sacrifice his son as a proof of faith and experienced G-d's compassion. *Bismillah ar-Rahman ar-Rahim*, In the name of G-d, the Compassionate, the Merciful, begins the first prayer in the Qur'an. There are ninety-nine names of G-d in Islam, each an attribute of the divine that humans can understand: the Compassionate, the Merciful, but also the Creator, the Seer, the Omniscient, the All Hearing, the Majestic, the Omnipotent, and ninety-one more, all portals through which G-d can be experienced. While there are ninety-nine listed in the Qur'an, Ibn al-Arabi says that, in fact, G-d has an infinity of names and attributes, like the stars in the sky. Only Allah, however, refers to nothing humans can understand; it is a marker for the unknowable, an aseity without human form or emotion.

Today I will do the Muslim pilgrimage. I will go to the third most important mosque in the world, after the ones in Mecca and Medina. I will go to the place where the Prophet Muhammad /pbuh/ went on his night journey from Mecca to Jerusalem and then ascended into heaven on his magical steed Buraq (a chimera, half woman, half horse) to greet all the Prophets and receive instructions from G-d. Mihraj: the ascension.

Jerusalem was taken by the Muslim caliph Umar around 635 CE and remained a Muslim city for 450 years. The Western Wall of Jerusalem (built in 19 BCE by Herod the Great) was added to during the Umayyad period. At this time, Muslim rulers were obliged to protect all the people of the covenant under their jurisdiction and grant them freedom to practice their religion (though sartorial distinction was required).

I meet my guide, Ahmed, outside my hotel. He is in his twenties and went to school in Germany for a time, so speaks

German, as well as English, Hebrew, and his native tongue, Palestinian Arabic.

I explain to Ahmed what I also explained to Avi and Adam—my mixed heritage at birth, then decades of intermittent practice with Sunni Sufis in Morocco and then France after marrying a secular Muslim man. I tell him I've prayed at the Umayyad Mosque as well as Ibn al-Arabi's tomb in Damascus, at the Great Mosque in Aleppo, the Koutoubia Mosque in Marrakech, and the Zawiya of Moulay Idriss II in Fès. I tell him I would like to pray at Al-Aqsa Mosque and at the even more sacred Dome of the Rock. As we walk toward the Muslim Quarter, he explains to me the several levels of security in place.

"It's hard to get in. First there are Israeli and Muslim guards. The Israeli guards are usually Druze by the way, the stateless minority loyal to the country that harbors them. After that, there are Muslims at the inner gate. They will ask you to say the prayers. And then, if you pass those two checkpoints, there are guards at the entrances of the Dome and the mosque. It's not easy."

"The tourist gate is crowded at this time," he tells me. "You can enter from this one." We walk toward one of the many Muslim gates as I try to go over the prayers in my head. It is Sunday morning at 8:30 a.m.—not time for prayer at the mosque. Still, I will need to perform my conversion just to get into the grounds.

Tourists are allowed into the compound but can only look at the buildings from the outside and walk in the surrounding gardens. They cannot enter what Jews call the "holy of holies," the place where the Ark of the Covenant was kept and where Solomon's Temple was destroyed, now under the Dome of the Rock. Ahmed reminds me that Jews would not enter even if they could, until the Messiah comes and the Third Temple is rebuilt. For that to happen, the Dome must fall. Fall or be transformed. Until that time, entering the grounds of the Temple Mount is taboo for Jews, which is why they pray outside, at the Western or Wailing Wall.

But who am I today? Is it pure hubris to choose? I am nervous. Doubt assails me as we walk toward the compound. If I am accused of being a fraud, or even if they don't let me in, am I breaking the law? Whose law, in fact, must I follow? The Jewish laws? All 613 of them? The Muslim sharia, which contains many dictums as well? Christ came, some believe, to replace all those rules with two: love G-d, and love thy neighbor as thyself. I can see the allure.

To assert freedom from the law is a kind of taking leave. But doesn't the law return with the force of social precedent, ever exceeding the individuals who inhabit its conventions? The Ten Commandments exist in all three religions. Breaking those, we transgress social taboos anchored in human consciousness. Break those, and the price is high: coveting the wife (or husband) of one's neighbor, stealing, lying, to say nothing of the other so-called abominations. Is this why on Yom Kippur Jews ask for forgiveness for sins they may not even have committed yet? Is leave taking from the law as inevitable as the social punishment it exacts? Stigma. Shame. Staying in one's designated lane instead of taking one's leave?

"They'll just turn you away," Ahmed assures me. "You won't go to jail or anything."

I resolve to enter, and almost immediately Ahmed stops.

"It's just ahead," he says. "You can't be seen with me as they know I'm a tourist guide. I'll wait here." And he turns down a side street, leaving me to go on alone, to walk into an unknown future, as so many converts do. And is not this the impetus, even the thrill of conversion—to wake in a new body of belief and sensate practice? A new body is a new world, I have always told my students. Imagining a new body is the privilege of (some) humans and the trade of writers like myself.

My fate has been sealed, and I walk on. Shafts of light illuminate the raffia-covered street, the shops still shuttered. I have already tied my scarf tightly around my head and under my chin, then around the back of my neck so no flesh shows. I crease the scarf around my ears and pull the cloth toward my forehead to conceal my hairline. I have learned to do this over many years of chanting with the Sufi sisters, the *faqirat*, in Morocco. But I've also covered myself like this when chanting with the Sufis in France, which I have been doing now for more than fifteen years. Not in the Massif Central where I met Camille, but in the south where the Arabs, then called Saracens by the Christians, conquered what was then Septimania around 717 CE. I bought a house in the region in 2006 and almost immediately found the same Sufi order with whom I practice in Morocco seeded in the soil of Languedoc-Roussillon. It continues to flourish to this day in what is, after all, its natural habitat: greater Andalusia.

I return to my home in Languedoc each year, its worn stone stairs leading from a vaulted ground floor to a room that overlooks the valley of the Vaunage. It was, an archaeologist once told me, a shepherd's house in the Middle Ages, its sheep sheltering in the earthen basement, the hay kept in the loft above, where I sleep in the increasing heat of summer, windows open to welcome the zephyr should it come, the night breeze that cools the limestone walls embedded with shells from the time when these stones were the seabed. The house is my seashell of dreams.

And though I practice with the *faqirat* in the region when I am there—most of them second-generation North African French citizens—the village where I live was also the last holdout of the Protestants during the religious wars. The Protestants, that minority in France, who refused the sovereign pontiff in Rome in order to practice their own form of ascetic Christianity. Though I learned about the history of the village only after I bought the house, this village, my village, also turns out to have been the ancestral home of my Huguenot forebears, who escaped oppression in southern France and went to Sweden in the sixteenth century. At least that's the family folklore on my mother's side.

Before my Huguenot ancestors fled the south of France, however, they may very well have known some of the Jews of the region, who were landholders in the Middle Ages, even holding political office in the neighboring village of Vauvert (then Posquières). The Jews were expelled in 1306, but they returned again to the region, trading in land, in old clothes, and in livestock, trading in one identity for another as Conversos, landing always temporarily in places, including the village where I now have a home, a crossroads for the three religions that have formed me. What magnetism pulls us back to where we nonetheless always are?

And now I am in Jerusalem, a place I never thought I'd be, the omphalos of the world. I am still dressed in a black tunic that falls below my knees. Not a common tourist, but then, not in Muslim dress either. There are no Muslim (or Orthodox Jewish) women in pants in Jerusalem, at least that I've seen.

"Are you a Muslim?" I am stopped by the first Israeli guard, a man in combat boots with an AK-47 slung over his shoulder. "What nationality are you?"

"American," I say, "but I lived in Morocco for many years. I married a Moroccan, and now live in the UAE."

"ID."

I get out my passport. He flips through the pages, then motions me on. I move toward the inner gate, where three un-uniformed men are sitting drinking tea from small glasses.

"*Arabi?*" they ask in Arabic.

I respond in Arabic.

"*Amerikaniyya*," I say in my North African accent, "*wa-lakin skunt fi al-Maghrib muda tawila*. . . . I'm American but I lived in Morocco for many years. I married and had a child there. My daughter is Moroccan."

"You know how to pray?"

I now recite the Fatiha, the opening prayer of the Qur'an, my head slightly bowed in an attitude of reverence. If I have learned anything by living in Morocco as long as I have, it's that gestures convey as much meaning as words. A tilt of the head, a lowering of the eyes, a hand over the heart. "A gesture narrowly divides us from chaos," Artaud once said. It is the case now.

"Put this on," the guard instructs when I finish my recitation, handing me an ankle-length green cotton skirt with a long yellow stripe on the side. This takes me aback. I did not expect to be given clothes to wear; after all, my body is fully covered. But it seems I can't go in to pray wearing pants, even if they are capacious. I should have realized. I step into the skirt and slip the band up to my waist. I'm sure I look ridiculous, but more importantly, I've been marked. Instead of a yellow star, I've been given a yellow stripe.

The guard from al-Waqf, the Jordanian Islamic protection agency responsible for controlling and managing this holy site, waves me along. It turns out that I have come in at Bab al-Maṭhara, the Ablution Gate, and the Dome is right before me. I am momentarily stunned; its turquoise and aquamarine mosaics, the calligraphy around its perimeter, the dome itself of dazzling gold. There are not too many tourists walking the grounds. It is still early, and the sky is a brilliant blue over the polished beige stone of the esplanade. I climb the stairs and walk toward the sanctuary, which seems to call me with a silent melody in my sternum.

Later, Ahmed will tell me that the Israelis agreed never to do any excavations on this site. Would the remains of the First Temple still be there? And the Second? Would the room that only the highest Jewish clerics could enter, the Holy of Holies, be found, along with the Ark of the Covenant? Is anything archaeologically exact in Jerusalem, or is it all myth and story? And does it matter at all? What's sure is that this wonder has been here since the Umayyad Empire ruled Jerusalem (661–750 CE) and is the oldest example of Islamic architecture in the world.

I reach the entrance and once again am stopped by a man at the threshold.

"Muslim?" he asks in Arabic. People here don't mince words. I tell him the same story that I told the Waqf guard at the last gate, reciting the Fatiha prayer, but this man wants more.

"What other prayers do you know?" he asks. I stumble. Of course, I know others, but it's been years since I've said them. Salat al-Tibbiya, Ayat al-Kursi. Where are those words now?

"I usually say the Fatiha when I pray," I tell him. He sees he has made me nervous and starts reciting Surah al-Ikhlas, one of the shortest prayers of Islam, the one that I saw when peeking in the mosque with Adam just yesterday. He waits for me to finish the sentence.

"*Qul: Huwa Allahu Ahad Allahu Samad* . . . Say, G-d is One, He is Eternal. . . ." But the following verse doesn't come to me right away.

"*Lam yalid* . . ." the guard continues.

And I finish, "*wa lam yulad*." Again, I freeze, and he steps in. "*Wa lam yakun lahu*. . . .

And then it comes back to me: "*kufuwan ahad*," I finish. "Say: He is G-d, the One and Only. G-d, the Eternal, Absolute. He begetteth not, nor is He begotten. And there is none like unto Him." It is the verse that asserts G-d's unicity, the one that defies the concept of the Trinity (Qur'an 112). In fact, such verses line the walls of the Dome in calligraphy.

"Allah!" one surah begins. "There is no god worthy of worship except Him, the Ever-Living, All-Sustaining. Neither drowsiness nor sleep overtakes Him. To Him belongs whatever is in the heavens and whatever is on the earth. Who could possibly intercede with Him without His permission? He fully knows what is ahead of them and what is behind them, but no one can grasp any of His knowledge—except what He wills to reveal. His Seat encompasses the heavens and the earth, and the preservation of both does not tire Him. For He is the Most High, the Greatest (Qur'an 2:255)."

"Go in," he says.

I breathe deep and manage a half smile. "Where do I leave my shoes?" I ask him.

"Take them with you," he says in Arabic, "in your hands."

I remove my shoes and go inside. The large slab of rock in the inner sanctum is surrounded by a wooden lattice. I put my shoes on a shelf by the wall, then peek through the slats to gaze at the stone, white with crevasses and smooth. I then walk the perimeter of this octagon, with its plush carpeting, its shining blue ceramics inlaid in geometrical shapes, calligraphy encircling the walls, its gold dome rising high above the sacrifice stone in the center.

It is quiet. I am one of five women in the Dome. These are tourist hours after all, and most of the tourists who come are not Muslim, so not allowed inside. Two women are praying, and I stand behind them, facing Mecca and Medina. Though the Prophet Muhammad /pbuh/ originally chose Jerusalem for the orientation of prayer. That changed with a revelation—or was it politics? I put my hands next to my ears, then drop my arms to my sides, and in a barely audible whisper I begin.

"*Allahu Akbar*." I fold my hands across my chest and say the Fatiha prayer under my breath, my tongue moving in rhythm with the words. Then in a half sigh, "*Allahu Akbar*," I fold my body to the carpeted ground and touch my forehead to the floor. *Allahu Akbar*, G-d is Greatest.

The peace that comes from attending fully to my body is not unlike yoga or meditation. The rug emits a subtle perfume, and the room is quiet, the fluctuation of my breathing the loudest thing in my ears as I bend my body forward toward the ground, the words I inhabit as easily as a sigh.

When I have done the required two prostrations, I sit on my heels and say the Ikhlas Prayer as I used to do when I prayed like this more regularly. Now it all comes back to me. "He is G-d, the One, the Eternal Refuge, He neither begets nor is born, nor is there to Him any equal." Then I pray once more for the souls of my departed parents and for the health and safety of my two children.

"*Salamu alay-kum*," I say, turning my head to the left. "*Salamu alay-kum*." I turn my head to the right. The angels of good and evil live on each side, and it is good to greet them both. Neither one exists without the other, and no one needs an unnecessary enemy.

I get up to leave when a woman approaches me. "*Salamu alay-kum*," she says.

"*Alay-kum salam*."

"Where are you from?" she asks in Arabic. I am getting used to these interrogations, beginning as they did at JFK Airport. I tell her the same story I have now repeated three times in twenty minutes, adding that it was a blessing for me to be able to pray at the Dome of the Rock. I am sincere. She smiles, seemingly satisfied, and wishes me peace once again. I go get my shoes, say good-bye to the guard outside the door, and make my way across the esplanade to Al-Aqsa Mosque, about fifty meters away. Here the shoe racks are outside the building, and I head toward them but am quickly stopped.

"Where are you going?" yet another guard says in English.

"I'm going to pray," I answer in Arabic, though he sees that I am clearly marked as a tourist, first by my style of dress (neither in a djellaba nor in a long dress) and second by this damning green skirt with the yellow stripe.

"Moroccan?" he asks, hearing my accent.

And once again I recount my story, not wanting to stray from my original narrative but also not wanting to stray from the truth. I was brought up never, ever to lie. It's in the Ten Commandments, of course, Exodus 20:16: "Thou shalt not bear false witness against thy neighbor." And in Proverbs 12:22: "Lying lips are an abomination to the Lord." And even in the Talmud: "The Holy One, blessed be He, hates a person who says one thing with his mouth and another in his heart" (Pesahim 113b). One needs to adhere to the truth, like a barnacle to the rock of Justice. Taking leave from the truth is a departure, a transgression.

I discovered when I lived in Morocco, however, that lying is more nuanced in the Islamic world. In one of the Hadith, the Prophet /pbuh/ is quoted as saying, "Lying is wrong except in three things: the lie of a man to his wife to make her content with him, a lie in war, for war is deception, or a lie to settle trouble between people" (Ahmad, 6.459). Apart from the clear chauvinism in this dictum, the saying acknowledges that fabrications are necessary to smooth social relations and that transparency is not always the best policy. Nonetheless, I could not, and did not want to lie now.

Again, I am asked to recite a prayer, just the Fatiha this time, and I am allowed to enter. But this time a man follows me in and stays by my side. Two men are napping against the walls of the mosque. Otherwise, it is just him and me inside.

"You want to pray?" the man asks me in heavily accented English. I nod and he brings me to the front of the room, next to the qibla against the eastern wall. And yet again, I pray, this time highly conscious that I am being observed.

Muslim prayer is not an intellectual activity for me, or not merely. It's in the body, in the movements and prostrations. The gestures correspond to basic human emotions, of devotion, of humility, of supplication. Genuflecting and praying on one's knees fulfills the same function in Catholicism. The

Protestants, in their austerity, do their best to erase the body from the equation. A big mistake, since devotion is a bodily act and leaves little room for doubt and speculation. You are in it or you are not. It is an attitude, a disposition, not a thought.

In the Qur'an (verse 49:14) there is a story about some Bedouins who profess to be believers, but the Prophet tells them, through divine revelation, "You have not yet attained to faith; you should rather say, We have submitted." Faith, *iman*, is a higher station than submission (*islam*), but it can only be attained through the portal of surrender, a taking leave of one's ego and hubris to follow a designated path. Submission is a bodily comportment. It is about giving one's body to G-d, and more aptly to the social order. Muslims share this with Jews.

Still, while I have known devotion, it is not my path. I can perform it, can repeatedly pray, but choosing one path over another is hard. The directions in which they lead somehow seem arbitrary in the end, as I always come back to the null point of existence, the absence at the heart of every presence, the axis in the center of every whirl. *Va vers toi et quitter la maison de ton père*. I take my leave.

As soon as I stand up from praying, the man is at my side holding a Qur'an.

"Here," he says, "write your name in the Qur'an and give a donation. Do you have children? Write their names too."

I am a bit overwhelmed. If he is being sincere, *mukhlis*, then I should follow his directions. Perhaps he thinks this will be a blessing. Perhaps he thinks I'm rich. I am not. But I do have three hundred dollars in shekels in my purse to pay my guide, Ahmed, and to take a taxi from Jerusalem to Ben Gurion airport in Tel Aviv tomorrow morning, a forty-minute trip. I open my wallet, and he sees the stack of bills. I give him fifty shekels, about thirteen dollars, but he looks at me askance.

"Write your name here, here," he says. And I begin to write my name in Arabic.

"No, no, in English," he insists.

And I do, as he's practically breathing down my neck.

"And your daughter's name too. And your parents. Now give me a hundred dollars."

"A hundred dollars?"

"For the mosque, for the mosque."

I reach into my wallet and draw out two more fifty-shekel notes.

"Give some more," he says.

I do as I'm told. Am I ensorcelled? Or simply afraid? Or is something else going on? In any case, I'm such an easy mark.

I think back to another instance when money and pilgrimage collided. I was visiting the sanctuary of Moulay Idriss II deep in the labyrinthine medina of Fès. Moulay Idriss II was a descendant of the Prophet Muhammad /pbuh/ and a major figure in the Islamization of Morocco. His shrine, with its mosaic tiles, carved stucco, black-and-white marble columns and large wooden dome, has been a pilgrimage site for those wishing to share in the baraka, or blessing, of this saint for centuries. Baraka is a material grace that resides in places like tombs, springs, or other holy sites. It also exists in the flesh of certain individuals, both during their lives and after their deaths. It is believed that the shaykh of the Sufi order, for example, can transmit it simply through his gaze.

I was there with my son, seventeen at the time, who is decidedly not Moroccan, and although I was dressed modestly, we were stopped by a man responsible for safeguarding the shrine. When we entered, he inquired as to who we were. I did not say that my son was Muslim, but I did recite my genealogy. He allowed us to approach the tomb and to take in the baraka of Sidi Moulay Idriss, but he, too, exacted an offering, a rather large sum, that he summarily pocketed.

The man in Al-Aqsa Mosque closes the Qur'an, and the money disappears.

"Come, follow me," he says, and I obey. "This is Salaheddine's minbar," he says. I nod in assent. "And this is the chamber of Maryam." We enter a small stone alcove. "And here," he says, moving on, "here is the Mihrab of Zakariyya."

He expects me to know what all this means, the history of the saints in this place, but I do not. I have not done my homework, and in any case, I am engulfed in my worries—*wiswas*, they are called in Arabic, the whisperings of Satan. Should I not be here?

He is saying something about the stained-glass windows and an earthquake, when he stops and says, "One hundred dollars for the tour."

I'm inwardly indignant, but my head is spinning and I am too insecure. I reach into my wallet and bring out more shekels.

"No, no. Dollars, you don't have dollars?"

"I have two twenties, that's all," I stammer, and he snatches them from my hand. I want to get out of here, but then I remember that I did not write my son's name in the Qur'an, not because I forgot, but because, following the truth of my narrative, only my daughter is Moroccan, not my son. But what if, I start to wonder, there is real baraka in this place? What if the names in the Qur'an are like the names in the Book of Life during Rosh Hashanah? Suddenly I am seized by superstition and have to add my son's name to the other inscriptions. The Qur'an is just where the man left it, on top of a pile that worshippers will use when they come to pray. He opens it again, and I add my son's name: Nathaniel. Like my own, it is a Jewish name, meaning the gift of G-d in Hebrew. And he is.

I head for the door, find my shoes, and start walking quickly away. Outside the sun bounces off the gold dome before me and, like Saul, I am temporarily blinded. There are more tourists than there were when I came, but the grounds are vast, and I walk to clear my head. My tour guide, Ahmed, must be wondering where I am. I look at my phone and find he has texted me several times. He is inside the compound, he says, but where am I? I text him a picture of my location, near Gate 7, the one that leads directly into the covered market. Markets and pilgrims have always existed together, but I know this time I've been fleeced.

A falsehood—if believed—creates a counternarrative, another truth. But what is the truth of the matter when one lives between categories, between meanings and symbols? Lies are dangerous because they reveal the chaos that always exists under the surface of human syntax, the danger, as anthropologist Mary Douglas observed, of being neither this nor that, impure, transitioning, refusing to be fixed in space, like the quanta on which all life is based. It is the lie of fixity that must be maintained for social life to proceed in an orderly manner. I believe that, don't I?

We walk past the Dome and sit on a small wall above the Golden Gate, sealed shut by Suleiman the Magnificent in 1541, perhaps because it's the only access to the Temple Mount from outside the medina, perhaps because it is said that when the

Jewish Messiah comes, he will arrive through that gate. Across from us, outside the walls, are the Mount of Olives, the Garden of Gethsemane, and the Jewish cemetery. Churches and mosques dot the hills, and no doubt synagogues, though they have neither minaret nor spire to pierce the sky. Jews have had to be more clandestine. Indeed, the oldest temple is not above but below the earth, under the very place where we sit, the First and Second Temple, the Holy of Holies. It is here, under the Dome of the Rock.

Ahmed and I walk to the olive grove in the north of the compound and watch young boys playing soccer on the grounds of the Islamic madrassa (the girls' school is on the southeast corner). He tells me that some of the stones upon which we are walking are more than two thousand years old. I look down at them, polished by the footsteps of the Romans, the Byzantines, the Umayyads, the Abbasids, the Crusaders, the Mamluks, the Ottomans, the British, and now the Palestinians and the Israelis (though not Orthodox Jews), as well as hordes and hordes of tourists from all over the world. These stones, washed by blood many times, in massacres. I add my footsteps to those, and like them, my life will disappear.

When we leave through Gate 7, I slip off the skirt that marks me as an outsider, and we enter the coolness of a medina street, sitting on stools at a juice bar where I tell Ahmed of my recent fleecing between sips of fresh pomegranate juice, its astringent sweetness soothing my nerves.

"You told them too much!" he exclaims. "The less you say, the better."

---

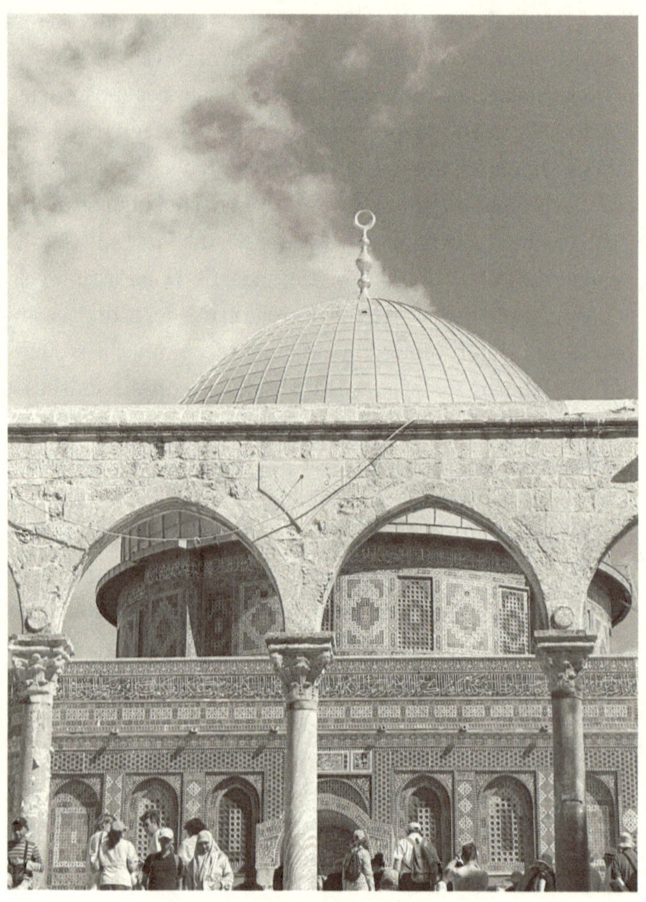

18 The Dome of the Rock. The golden dome covers the rock on which Muslims believe Abraham was ready to sacrifice his son. Jews believe that the Second Temple is also in this sacred place. (Photo: Deborah Kapchan)

To them will I give in my house and within my walls a memorial and a name [*yad vashem*] better than sons and daughters; I will give them an everlasting name, that shall not be cut off from memory.

וְנָתַתִּי לָהֶם בְּבֵיתִי וּבְחוֹמֹתַי יָד וָשֵׁם טוֹב מִבָּנִים וּמִבָּנוֹת; שֵׁם עוֹלָם אֶתֶּן לוֹ, אֲשֶׁר לֹא יִכָּרֵת.

**Isaiah 56:5**

"How you end your trip is most important," my friend Galit told me after hearing about how it began at JFK.

"Yes, it's how you *end* it that matters," her husband Freddie agreed.

I think there is a hidden meaning here, but I'm not sure what it is. Still, it sticks in my brain, and I feel compelled to traverse the new city and understand. It's my last afternoon in Jerusalem, and I go to Yad Vashem, the Holocaust Museum on Mount Herzl.

Ahmed accompanies me outside Jaffa Gate, buys me a ticket, and puts me on the correct tram. I ride with Orthodox women in dowdy clothes, with Orthodox men sweating in their black suits, their hats in their hands, and I notice that there are very few Palestinians. I get off at Mount Herzl and walk the path down a forested hill to the museum. Admission is free, and I enter, situating myself between two tour groups, one a regiment of young Israeli soldiers in fatigues without guns, the other Italian Jews.

The very first room documents the rise of anti-Semitism throughout history, and particularly before World War II. I stand in front of a documentary video detailing the enmity of Christians for Jews, something I never felt in my mixed family at all. For if Christ was destined to be sacrificed as the lamb of G-d, he could not have been murdered, since it was preordained. What's more, Christ himself was a Jew. And yet the video emphasizes that anti-Semitism arose in Christian populations. And who can deny that? Christians are being demonized for demonizing Jews. Wasn't it a crazed egomaniac who started it all? But no, anti-Semitism long predated Hitler.

It all seems so hopeless, the identitarian politics, the tribal hatred, the claims to land one cannot own. I want to scream with Carl Jung that the demon is inside. It's human barbarism, our own shadow self that we can't abide, and so project onto some Other who we believe is not us. It's the worm in our own apple, the abject child disgusted by its own bile. But then there are those who think that Jung himself was taken up by the verve of Hitler's government, and others who say he saw it for what it was after a short while. Who is immune to the mass hysteria of one's own time? In the Shoah, non-Jews who fought against the tide came later to be called the Righteous Among the Nations.

I walk through every room, ingesting as much as I can: the testimony of the survivors on video screens, the photographs of train cars packed with people on their way to Auschwitz, the documentation of the uprising in the Warsaw ghetto, the impossible will to create art in Terezin. Children's shoes in large piles, the material remains of hundreds of thousands of lives, in Chelmno, Treblinka, Sobibor, Belzec, Auschwitz-Birkenau, and Majdanek-Lublin. The documentation is meticulous and horrifying. Deportations from Belgium, France, Greece, Italy, Hungary, Norway, the Netherlands, and Romania. The farther I walk, the more paralyzed I become by the evil that exists in the world and in the human psyche.

Finally, I come to the Hall of Names, a symbolic burial ground for those who had no funeral, a place where millions of short biographies are stored, and where the nameless dead are also honored. A genizah. To lose one's name is to be lost to history, I think. Or does memory, like baraka, reside in the very ground where our genetic code disintegrates and from there arise again? It occurs to me then that the meaning of *aliya*, understood as the right of return, in fact comes from the word *ali*, "high" in both Hebrew and Arabic. Aliya is not just a movement back to the land of one's ancestors, but an ascent to the Temple Mount in Jerusalem, itself a symbol for what Spinoza might call the transition to a greater state of perfection. Jerusalem is that in its ideal form: the heavenly Jerusalem of the mind, a utopia.

I enter the last hall, a dark empty room of silence where poems, proverbs, and letters of the dead scroll across a screen. And there I break, sobbing quiet tears.

Once outside, I find myself before the rolling hills of Jerusalem. I take out my phone and text Galit a photo, so she knows where I am.

"No words," I write, "and yet words are all we have."

A minute later she answers, "Yes, and the endless sky. That is the only thing that can embrace the voices and the silences that you heard and those that echo through you afterwards."

The way you end your trip is most important. I end mine here, among the persecuted.

I go back to my hotel, skipping dinner, and pack the few things I have in my carry-on. I take some notes, but mostly I just lie on the hotel bed and think. And then a text comes from Galit.

"I was speaking to my colleagues at the Hebrew University," she writes. "They think you might have trouble at the border when leaving. Make sure that this time you say you are Jewish. And check your email. I am sending you a letter thanking you for your talk at the Institute, as well as the poster for the conference that has your name in Hebrew. Show it to the guards, if they give you any trouble."

Trouble. It's not something I am used to having. Not that sort, at least. I usually slip quietly around political dissonance. But now I am worried. I wrote my name in that Qur'an after all, a Jewish name in a Muslim holy book, in a place where only Muslims are permitted. And yet I am leaving as a Jew through the security border. And my UAE visa, should anyone check, has me down as a Christian expatriate. Who, or what, in fact, am I? And why must I choose?

"Some people cannot choose," a rabbi in Abu Dhabi would say to me soon after my return. They are born Jews, and Jews they remain. But by that logic, I too cannot choose. I am a hybrid, born to live in between. It's not always a comfortable place to be.

When I arrive at the airport, I face the same questions I got six days before.

"What holidays do you celebrate?" the security guard asks.

"I'm secular," I say once more.

"Yes, but what holidays can you name?"

"Passover," I say.

"And what do you do on Passover?"

"Well, I don't celebrate it often." I joke, "I hate gefilte fish. But the youngest at the table asks questions, we eat matzah, bitter herbs, you know . . ."

The guard smiles. "Move on," she tells me.

"Shalom," I proffer.

## The Heavenly Jerusalem

Friend, hope for the Guest while you are alive.

—**Kabir,** fifteenth-century Indian mystic

Hopeless heart that thrives on paradox . . .

—**Jeanette Winterson,** *The Passion*

I SIT IN A WICKER ROCKER on the terrace of my apartment in Abu Dhabi, looking across the blue-green estuary before me. It is September, still very warm in the Gulf, and the date palms and *ghaf* trees wave gently on the patch of lawn between me and the shore. I sit here for hours sometimes, computer on my lap, dog curled up in his bed by my side, writing and watching the boats and ferries stream past. I've never seen dolphins on this stretch, but there are plenty nearby.

I live on the island called Saadiyat, Happiness. In contrast to the main island, downtown Abu Dhabi, with its skyscrapers towering over the corniche, Saadiyat is the cultural district, home to the lattice-domed Louvre and the Abrahamic Family House, a complex of three centers of worship—the Moses Ben Maimon Synagogue, the Saint Francis Catholic church, and the Imam Ahmed El-Tayeb Mosque, all connected with a shared marble esplanade. A menorah, a cross, and a crescent moon rise from each of three pinnacles, illuminating the interfaith sky. Soon the Zayed National Museum and the Guggenheim will be completed, all designed by internationally acclaimed architects. There's a neighborhood called Mamsha five minutes away where one can dine in the open air, drinking alcohol while watching bikini-clad bathers on the crystalline beach.

My own Saadiyat neighborhood is more residential. Dotted with five-story rental units overlooking both sea and estuary, it is landscaped with frangipani trees and grass-lined walkways bordered by an array of small flowering bushes that bloom all year: purple phlox, clusters of tender white alyssum, flaming red dragon-wing begonias, pink petunias, and storksbill pelargonium. A patch of snapdragons, their white lips surrounding violet tongues, flutters gently in the breeze outside my building, and Star-of-Bethlehem, also called Arabian starflower, wafts its heady jasmine-like odor up from the ground. When I walk around the island each day with my dog, a saluki mix, I remember how lucky I am to be in a country with extremely low crime rates, mild winters, and a cultural scene lively enough to keep me more than busy in the evenings.

Still reeling from all I experienced in Israel, I plan to celebrate the Jewish High Holidays in the first synagogue in the United Arab Emirates, and while I could have stayed in Jerusalem for Rosh Hashanah and the ten holy days of atonement that culminate in the fast on Yom Kippur, I want to be here in Abu Dhabi with a group of Jews who, like me, are declaring themselves publicly in this Arab country for the first time.

When I first moved to Abu Dhabi in 2018, it was because my adolescent son was taking risks in Manhattan that his fifteen-year-old brain couldn't corral. I had to get him out of the city, to take leave of that reality and enter another, this time for his sake. My university in New York has a campus in Abu Dhabi, and I asked for a temporary transfer. Temporary was not to be, however. At least I am still here today.

Soon after my arrival, I am invited to join a WhatsApp group for Jews in the UAE by a friend of a friend from graduate school. I give him my number—why not?—and I begin to regularly peruse the group chat, including enthusiastic responses to the Abraham Accords, a document signed in September 2020 by the UAE, the United States, Bahrain, and Morocco, promoting, as the document says, "interfaith and intercultural dialogue to advance a culture of peace among the three Abrahamic religions and all humanity."

The Accords officially recognize Israel and establish diplomatic as well as economic relations between the signatory countries. Direct flights from Abu Dhabi to Tel Aviv are established, and we watch as the Abrahamic Family House is built. That year I celebrate the High Holidays with the Hasidim, along with many other expatriates—Jews who in their home countries of France, Italy, Russia, the UK, and the United States would probably never attend Hasidic services—lining up before a table with candles, praying that we and our loved ones be inscribed in the book of life for another year.

*Bah-rookh ah-tah Ah-doh-noi Eh-loh-hay-noo Meh-lekh hah-oh-lam.* . . . Blessed are you, L-rd our G-d, king of the universe, who has sanctified us with his commandments, and has commanded us to kindle the light of the Day of Remembrance. . . .

One day, I receive an invitation to a wedding (by text), the nuptials of Rabbi Levi Duchman and his bride, Lea Hadad. It will be held at the Hilton, a thirty-minute drive from Saadiyat, on the neighboring island of Yas. It is, the invitation says, the first official Jewish wedding in the UAE since the Abraham Accords. And though I know no one, though I will walk in alone (the only woman among 1,500 guests to wear pants), I decide to attend.

On the day of the wedding (September 14, 2022), I pull my economy car up to the hotel and, as I am handing the keys to the valet, notice a couple and their toddler going through a metal detector at the front door. Of course security is tight, I tell myself. This is a Jewish wedding in an Arab country after all, and not everyone approves of the Abraham Accords. I also notice that both the man and his wife are wearing the clothes of the Chabad-Lubavitchers, a branch of Hasidim with centers all over the world, the man in a black suit with ritual tassels hanging at his side, his wife in a long-belted dress and wearing a wig. In fact, the wedding is an orthodox Hasidic wedding.

That evening I am stirred to the core. Something about the sacred piyyutim of Eastern Europe, sung by a group of men in long black coats, makes me ache for my father, dead these twenty years. Something about the prayers, said over and over for centuries, the groom davening as he walks down the aisle, the veiled bride circling him seven times, spins my own heart on its axis. But there is something else: the context. Jews dancing the hora with Arab Muslims in gandouras. It is historic, a small opening, perhaps, to peace in the Middle East. (Such tenuous openings, I will be reminded soon afterward, are always poised to re-close.)

A few weeks after the wedding, I meet the rabbi in a coffee shop. He tells me that he has lived in Morocco long enough to learn Moroccan Arabic, and we exchange some words in that most particular of Arab variants. I tell him about my mixed heritage, how my mother converted to Judaism to marry my father but never practiced despite the fact that she believed the Jews were the chosen people, how I was brought up between faiths, going on to do "research" on Moroccan Sufism for decades. I tell the rabbi enough for him to know that I am first and foremost a mystic, a seeker of the *experience* of divinity. I am curious about what that means in Judaism. So I begin to read some of the works of Rabbi Menachem Mendel Schneerson, one of the most revered leaders of the Chabad-Lubavitcher movement. Through his works, I understand that he and his followers believe that divinity is omnipresent, that it is the job of humans to become conscious of that. Animals have souls and people can change their destinies, not only narrating a future but transforming the past, since time itself is also a mystery. For the Lubavitchers, I learn, G-d is immanent in all things. They are, like many mystics throughout history (Sufi and non), monist and panentheistic.

Schneerson had also been to Morocco and exhorted Jews to stay in the Arab lands of their birth. In his pictures on the web, he looks like my grandfather, Nathan Kapchan, round face, white hair, blue eyes. And like my grandfather, he came from Ukraine. Was my Grandpa Nat also a follower of the Baal Shem Tov, Israel ben Eliezer, the one who knew the secret name of G-d?

I'd explored my Judaism once before, at a synagogue in the United States where the rabbi made it clear that I would always be an outsider because my mother was not *born* Jewish. I did not stay long. But this time something else is moving within me. I read about the Kabbalah, about how there is nothing but the Infinite, the Ein Sof, disclosed in the physical realm through divine emanations, *sefirot*. I read about Shekhinah, the attribute of the divine feminine, that resides in nature and travels in everyone and everything. Shekhinah comes from the root *sa/ka/na* in both Hebrew and Arabic: to dwell or inhabit. It's the word used for spirit possession in Morocco. Spirits dwell in the body, as the sacred dwells in all things. We are always multiple.

After my baptism in the Protestant church as a newborn, after thirty years of practicing remembrance ceremonies, *dhikr*, with Sufis in Morocco and France, I feel as if I've come back to a place I never really left. *Teshuvah*, it's called in Hebrew. Although many equate this with repentance, it literally means "return." Not only a return to G-d, but a return to the state of one's birth, to an essential wisdom, the thing humans innately possess but have forgotten. (It's called *fitra* in Arabic, humans' innate nature and knowing of G-d.)

And yet how likely is such a return here in the Arab Gulf, in the Emirate of Abu Dhabi? Henri Bergson, the great French philosopher, who died at the height of World War II and the Vichy government, wrote this in his last will and testament in 1937, when anti-Semitism was cresting in Europe: "My reflections have brought me closer and closer to Catholicism, where I see the complete fulfillment of Judaism. I would have converted if I had not seen the formidable wave of anti-Semitism brewing for years which will sweep over the world. I want to remain among those who will be persecuted tomorrow."

Unlike Bergson, I have been taking *leave* of my Christian roots most of my life, but I am galvanized by his words, *J'ai voulu rester parmi ceux qui seront demain des persécutés.* "I want to remain among those who will be persecuted tomorrow." What is it about minority status that takes such hold of the imagination? In Abu Dhabi, a desire awakens in me to live this historic moment as a Jew, to attend the first synagogue in this part of the Arab Muslim world. I am drawn to my Judaism in a way I have not been before. Is it the many years of reading Hannah Arendt and Adorno, Spinoza, Bergson, Levinas, Benjamin, Cixous, and Derrida? I resonate with the critical tradition of these thinkers, although, and perhaps because, many of them are secular, even heretics in the eyes of the faith. But am I not always identified as a Jew by others, because of my name and my physical type? Would I not also, with my father, have been sent to the ovens? From what in fact *can* we take our leave, and what sticks to our very cells like epigenetic glue?

In September 2023, I arrive at the newly opened Moses Ben Maimon Synagogue before sunset and enter the sanctuary, touching the mezuzah and bringing my fingers to my lips. A wooden trellis, a *mechitza*, separates the women's section from the men's, and I take my seat on the pew behind the visiting rabbi's wife, an elegant woman whose silver hair is partially covered by a pillbox hat. I follow her movements, standing and sitting where appropriate, taking the three steps backward after the Kaddish prayer to symbolize the three *mils* the

Jews retreated after hearing the sound of G-d upon giving the Torah to Moses on Mount Sinai; symbolizing also the three heavenly partitions, between Moses and G-d. With the rabbi's wife, I turn toward the back of the synagogue to welcome the Sabbath, the "bride," at sunset.

As the rabbi begins the service, chanting a psalm, the Muslim call to prayer floats into the room from the neighboring mosque. *There is no G-d but G-d*. The two sounds of worship collide and spin upward from the bimah into the atrium. If this were a church, the sounds would echo in the apse, but above our heads is a tall voluminous cube draped with golden mesh, meant to symbolize Abraham's tent. The netting cascades down on four sides, sheltering the congregation in its girth.

In all the years I spent in Morocco, I never came out as a Jew. I watched as little children threw stones at a middle-aged Jewish couple in the town where I lived. As owners of a thriving grocery, they hadn't left for Israel or Canada like most other Jews did. They had the best prices in town. They had to. Still most Moroccans felt nothing but enmity toward Israel and the way it treated Palestinians in the territories. The conflation of state and people was too easy to make. Pan-Arab sentiment was palpable, especially after the Arab defeats in 1967. And although my Moroccan mother-in-law came from a tribe called Ait Ichou, purportedly a Jewish name, there was no memory of Muslim conversion in the family, or if there was, it wasn't discussed. So, I lay low. After all, my Jewish family in New York also had their prejudices. So much depended on where you were born and grew up.

My mother in fact never let me attend the High Holidays with my Jewish family. She thought I would be lured off the path of Christianity. And she was right. I would have been, since my

Jewish family knows who they are. They are funny, not tragic like my northern European side (whose temperaments veer more toward characters in Ingmar Bergman films). When looking at family photos with my older cousin in Los Angeles on a recent trip, I comment on my absence at the holiday gatherings.

"My mom never wanted me to be at Passover," I remark. "She was afraid I'd become . . ."

"Who you are now!" he exclaims loudly, finishing my sentence. We both laugh. It seems I've, indeed, taken leave only to return, decades later, to a place I have never really left at all. Teshuvah.

*Le judaïsme est un club dont on ne peut pas démissionner*, "Judaism is a club from which one cannot resign," my close friend and colleague Phillipe Gaudin once said, citing the Jewish scholar George Steiner. I did my ritual induction late in life, but this does not negate the fact that it has been with me since my beginnings in the womb of my mother. For how many Jews descend from mixed marriages? Abraham himself, the common ancestor of all three religions, wed Hagar and Keturah after Sarah's death, both converts to Judaism. King Solomon is said to have had more than a thousand wives and concubines, most of them foreign. Does my Celtic and French Huguenot blood negate that I am also 50 percent Ashkenazi, or that my father's eastern European cells migrated to my mother's womb, taking up residence not only in me but in her own body for decades after she gave birth? For it turns out that after parturition, a mother is henceforth a chimera, a being with two distinct gene sets. We humans are a porous lot.

The term *Hebrew*, I read, may derive from the word *'eber*, or *'ever*, meaning "other side." Just as Abraham crossed the

Euphrates into the land of Canaan, the Jews have been crossing divides, both geographic and genetic, since the time of the First Temple. Some in fact think that all Ashkenazi Jews were originally converts and not part of the twelve tribes.

Islam was not my genetic heritage. It was a choice, or so it felt. The last religion, according to its practitioners—one that accepts all the prophets of Christianity and Judaism—it provided a kind of resolution to the tear in my given identities. Yet there are some things that may be immutable, at least in the span of a human life: atoms, carbon, sound waves, light. At the subatomic level, aren't we all the same? Aren't we in fact all microchimeras, symbolic Buraqs taking imaginal flights in the stories that emerge from our very cells to write us into the book of life?

On a morning in October, just a few weeks after my return from Israel, I look at the WhatsApp chat. It's called Beit Tefilah, the house of prayer, a synonym for a synagogue, a virtual community of worship. Someone posted a video. Normally I would not look at it right away, but I see it's from Israel. I press play and watch a recording from just a few hours before. It is shot from someone's window and shows snipers on the roof of a neighboring apartment building. Masked and dressed in black, they are shooting from the roof. I hear a little girl's voice in the video, frantically calling for her mother. And then the camera pans down to an open pickup truck with six men standing on its bed; they fire their machine guns at a passing car, killing everyone inside, then jump down and begin shooting indiscriminately on the street. People fall. Immobile bodies are splayed on the sidewalk. Screams. The picture goes black. This is how I learn of the October 7 attacks.

In the days to follow, I will watch more videos on the chat. Vigils in different parts of the world—Paris, Italy, London. Photos of empty chairs at a Shabbat dinner to symbolize the absent hostages. Organizations accepting donations for the families of the victims, for the soldiers going off to Gaza. There is discussion about whether to take one's mezuzah off the door lintel in Abu Dhabi. Someone posts a newspaper article about the UAE's continuing support for Israel and exhorts the community to remain calm. A police detail is stationed permanently in front of the synagogue.

I call Galit in Jerusalem, who is sheltering in her house with Freddie. There are sirens, she says, but that is all. They are planning to go to the United States and spend a few months with their grown children as soon as they can. I contact Avi, who has been called up for military duty. The rabbi's daughter is also in the army, and so are the grandchildren of some other friends. I think of my twenty-one-year-old son in the United States and how I used to put him to bed with a prayer, planting the seed that he never go and fight someone else's war.

Meanwhile in New York City, protests explode. Pictures of the hostages are plastered over buildings only to be torn down and replaced with posters: "From the river to the sea, Palestine will be free." Netanyahu's response is beyond the pale. With every passing day, the number of Palestinian deaths rises dramatically, far surpassing the number of Israeli victims—civilians, children, people with no skin in the game other than to survive each day. The aggression is unfathomable as Netanyahu's endgame becomes clear. Among the uncountable dead, Palestinian poets and journalists are killed in Gaza while Muslim youth are attacked indiscriminately. Jewish students and professors are singled out as unwitting perpetrators in the United States. I agonize about whether to sign letters calling for a ceasefire, not because the need for an immediate end to the violence is disputable, but because I doubt letters do anything but create a feeling of false agency in the signer, as well as a sense of unearned righteousness. One friend signs and is immediately called out as an anti-Semite on a public website. He has to hire a lawyer to get his name removed.

It has become current practice for intellectuals in the United States to begin public talks with an acknowledgment that the "land" they stand on once "belonged" to a native American tribe, the Lenape in Manhattan, for example, the Passamaquoddy in Maine. I find this practice specious. No one owns the land. Rather, one should say, "Here is the blood of the Lenape. Their DNA saturates and lives in this soil. Here they died. Here our ancestors killed them to occupy the land. Here we slaughtered, pillaged, coveted, raped, and thieved. Here we sinned." Teshuvah.

In February, four months after the horrors of October 7, a woman in the Jewish community gave birth to her second child, a son, and the Moses Ben Maimon Synagogue in Abu Dhabi held its first naming ceremony.

"A baby in the womb is like a folded notebook," the newly hired rabbi would say at the ceremony. "In the womb, some believe, a child has full knowledge of the Torah. It's blissful, the most blissful state of life. It's union after all. But before a child is born, an angel arrives, strikes it above the upper lip, where humans henceforth have a divot, and makes one forget everything. We spend our lives trying to remember what we already know."

In Arabic, the word for compassion and the word *uterus* come from the same root: *ra/ha/ma*. Womb, the source of compassion, but also the source of gnosis, the place where DNAs mix and novelty is born.

As a metaphor for G-d—for all we have are metaphors—light is the most ubiquitous. It is present in the Torah and in the Qur'an, in the Kabbalah and in the esoteric texts of the Christians. Christ is the light of the world, after all (John 8:12). And what is light but energy that is visible, electromagnetic waves vibrating at a frequency that humans can see? But there are many frequencies—most in fact—that remain invisible to the human eye: radio waves, microwaves, infrared radiation, ultraviolet rays, X-rays, and gamma rays, to name those scientists have defined. And what others might exist that we can't measure yet? We have no trouble believing that light travels from distant galaxies through space, that it is composed of separate particles (photons) that nonetheless travel as ceaseless waves, that by its very nature, light defies what humans have so far understood about the laws of the universe. And yet with three color receptor cones in our eyes and vision between 380 and 700 nanometers, humans see only 0.00035 percent of the entire electromagnetic spectrum. We are blind to most things.

When my body flooded with light as I meditated in my East Village studio so long ago now, what part of the electromagnetic spectrum was I glimpsing? When I heard the voice telling me that the man in the north was waiting for me, whose voice was I hearing? When Sidi Mimoun stood before me, telling me that "they," the spirits, "would win out," what message was he conveying? How to interpret all that? Revelation? Or simply the disclosure of my imagination to myself? Or rather *an* imagination that lives between minds and bodies, places and things?

Taking leave has always felt like a practice to me, a conscious method, an intervention in what might be called destiny. But perhaps my genetic heritage impelled me all along to the paths that I followed: to France to meet Camille, to North Africa, which was *his* dream, to Sufism, a living mysticism in a rational age, and back home to who I have been all along, the ten-year-old in a charnel ground who dreamed about writing a story.

I often think back to that day in the church cemetery waiting for my father to arrive. Sometimes he'd take me to the butcher shop, sides of beef hanging headless in the refrigerator waiting to be sectioned, the smell of schmaltz and blood in the air, wood shavings on the floor so people would not slip on the slick fat that seemed to be everywhere. I sat on a chair, watching him chop, knives of all sizes hanging on the wall, the wood block indented and regularly wiped. He wrapped the cuts in waxed paper before he handed them over the counter to the Jewish women, immigrants speaking Yiddish, or English with a Yiddish accent. How many years would I be a vegetarian to repent from what I perceived as those sins, his bloody apron and steel-toed shoes ever in my mind? How many times would I shy away from telling others what my father did for a living, my father the pacifist who couldn't hurt a soul, a man who in a blizzard walked from Yonkers to the Bronx at 3 a.m. just to open the store for his hungry customers?

Today, however, I think of my father differently. He is, for me, the butcher Carver Ting about whom the Chinese poet and philosopher, Chuang-Tzu, wrote. Carver Ting was a follower of the Tao whose "every touch of the hand, every inclination of the shoulder, every step he trod, every pressure of the knee, while swiftly and lightly he wielded his carving-knife, was as carefully timed as the movements of a dancer in the *Mulberry Wood. . . .*"

> There are spaces in the joints;
> The blade is thin and keen:
> When this thinness
> Finds that space
> There is all the room you need!
> It goes like a breeze!

Carver Ting knew about the interstices, the spaces in between. Like my mother, he was a dancer in the woods of imagination, finding the expanse between the joints, the thinness in a breeze.

It would be a good story to say that I was fated to come to Abu Dhabi to discover my Judaism. And while that may be true in part, I am still as deeply moved by the call to prayer as by the aching cry of the shofar. The masses and requiems Bach wrote for the church move me into realms of the sublime. Beauty is in fact what calls me, not a profession of faith. And beauty for me is in the slip between categories, the space between identities. It is the deliverance of the pen, and its path across the page.

My mother's religion was love. She did it imperfectly of course. But for her, it was what we were on earth to learn. She believed that the Jews were the chosen people. Chosen for what and by whom is a question that still haunts me. But for her it was clear: chosen by G-d to stand apart. She gave me that by marrying my father. And although it cost her her dance career, she insisted until her death that she never had regrets. A slight prevarication perhaps, but one done for love.

She used to dance with me before the large mirror in our Pelham Road apartment. On the orange wall-to-wall carpet, next to the faux-wood vinyl bar, she played the part of the man—she knew how to dance both parts—and taught me to listen to her body as she led me into steps on the tips of my toes. "Relax your arm," she said. "Feel where we are going. Slow, slow, quick, quick. Good. Now speed it up."

To dance with another is to be sensitive to their breath, to the way one body moves and the other responds. Eventually it is a duet. Sometimes one leads, sometimes one follows. This is the baraka, the grace of the dance, the lesson that movement is our only home. The space between the joints is where I reside. It is my Jerusalem, my *Bayt al-Maqdis*, my Dome of the Rock, my holy of holies. When I am not conscious of this, I am in exile.

To be human is to inhabit a style, a modality: a scarved head, a wig, a long or short dress. Each style is a *tzimtzum*, a mini-contraction, a particular manifestation of the one flesh of the world. G-d, the story goes, fashioned Adam out of clay, and clay, like all form, is subject to entropy. But energy, as it says of G-d in the Ikhlas Surah, is neither begotten nor does it give birth, it is neither created nor able to be destroyed. When waves act like particles and particles act like waves—as experiments in quantum physics demonstrate—are they also possessed, able to transform into what they are not, and yet somehow remain who they are? *Huwa/laysa Huwa*. Wave and not wave. Jew and not Jew. We are all that.

"Some people don't have a choice," the rabbi had insisted. We were sitting at the open-air café on the esplanade that con-

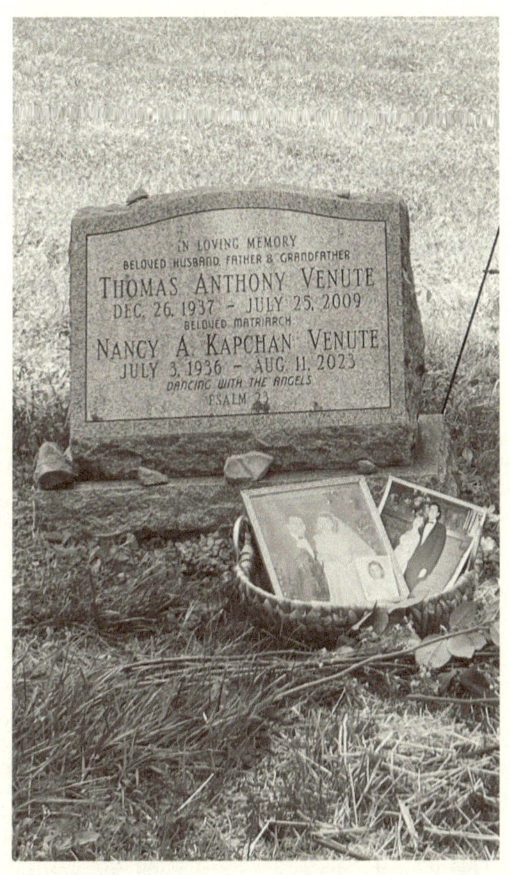


**19** "Dancing with the Angels." Nancy's headstone, with her two married names and photographs of her weddings with each of her two husbands. (Photo: Deborah Kapchan)

nects the synagogue with the church and the mosque, drinking a sweet hibiscus tea with rose petals floating on top. As the muezzin called out the *asr* prayer, I told the rabbi how I no longer felt the need to confess or apologize for my halfie status, that I now understood that Jews throughout history have been born from Gentile mothers, that converts, in fact, are numerous, sometimes lauded as the most Jewish of Jews.

This is when he said, "Yes, but some people don't have a choice." He was talking, I think, not so much about conversion as about those who are defined not only as Jews but as social pariahs, people that history defines as the less-than-human other. The people who inhabit this classification change—Armenians, Jews, Kurds, Mexicans, Palestinians, Uyghurs—but the category itself is perennial. No one chooses it. It is assigned.

Or do we choose it on some unconscious level and then immediately forget? Do all humans eventually cycle through both victor and victimhood in metempsychosis, or perhaps in one of the many other dimensions that string theory posits? Did my mother have a choice when she took leave of her Christianity and submerged herself in the mikvah? Did my father when he was drafted in the Korean War? Did I choose to delve into the mystical realms of a Sufi order when I lived in Morocco in 1994? Theological debates about free will and predestination aside, mathematics tells us it is a matter of probability. The likelihood of life veering in a certain direction is strong, but there is always the chance in a million or more that one escapes the assumed trajectory, that a particle turns in an unexpected direction and with it, the wave of destiny changes.

The word *leave*, after all, is also related to the word *belief*, and to the Middle English *beleave*, to desert or abandon. It is only when one leaves one's beliefs behind that one can know anything at all.

I never felt called to go to Israel. Although I understood, still understand, the longing for a haven of safety against the terrors of anti-Semitism, yet the brutal tragedies of what Palestinians call the Nakba, the catastrophe, in the 1948 Arab-Israeli War, as well as the horrific ongoing onslaughts ever since, have always been abhorrent to me. How can a state based on a religion be a democracy? That, and the eschatology of all three religions of the book—in which a war in Jerusalem precedes the messianic age, the return of Christ, and the day of judgment—all this made the place sound, well, frankly, meshugga, insane. Without these apocalyptic stories, would there still be the extreme strife in which humans, and particularly the Palestinians, now find themselves?

I never wanted to go to Jerusalem, but once there, the stones spoke to me. The tawny-white dolomitic limestone that paves the streets, and that rises above them, walling both the old city and the new, the density of history embedded in their slow obstinacy as witnesses to history, geology outliving human folly. The dry hills and the olive trees that border the city, the gates through which so many lives have passed.

One can't argue with place. It's a feeling, an inaudible sound rising up from the ground. The word in Hebrew is *makom*, a sacred space, as well as a name for G-d. Like *maqam* in Arabic, a spiritual station and a musical scale, places are both physical and spiritual states. They have a taste. We live in them, and yet they inhabit *us*, their melodies traversing our very bones, that themselves return to and nourish the soil. We can only listen, as we vibrate to their tune.

Jerusalem. Muslims call it *Bayt al-Maqdis*, the holy house. It is the place where the Prophet Muhammad /pbuh/ ascended into heaven, a place of passage, a portal to another realm. In a midrash, Jerusalem is defined as a composite of *yireh*—abiding place—and *salem*—peace, but the name may also derive from the word *shalem*, wholeness, while *yiru* is the Hebrew word for "[they] will see." Yirushalem, a vision of wholeness to come, a longing for completion, for what in Islam is called *tawhid*, unity with G-d in the *New* Jerusalem, the heavenly one.

William Blake evoked the heavenly Jerusalem in 1808 in what is now known as his prophetic books:

> I will not cease from Mental Fight
> Nor shall my sword sleep in my hand
> Till we have built Jerusalem
> In England's green and pleasant Land.

Unlike the earthly Jerusalem, the heavenly Jerusalem is a utopia of justice and peace, a place (*makom*/*maqam*) where all peoples and nations will one day meet, a city that will be renamed Yah·weh šām·māh, the Lord is there. For Blake, it is built by human hands. In the Book of Revelations, however, the heavenly Jerusalem descends as a woman "prepared as a bride adorned for her husband." It is a city of jasper, sapphire, chalcedony, emerald, sardonyx, carnelian, chrysolite, beryl, topaz, chrysoprase, jacinth, and amethyst; its gates of pearls; its streets of gold. Within her gemstone walls, there will no longer be tears nor death, sorrow nor pain, for "the former things are passed away," and the world will be new. For Christians, as well as Jews and Muslims, Jerusalem is the cosmic tree, its roots in the dirt, its trunk on the earth, its branches stretching upward into the ether. Jerusalem is what religious scholar Mircea Eliade called the *axis mundi*: the place between the material and the imagined, the vile and the righteous, the base and the most supreme. If the people of the three religions of the book stopped believing in this place, what would change?

A land can possess us. But humans cannot possess a land. We are renters on earth, as the late philosopher Michel Serres asserts. Possession is necessarily malfeasance, and yet nations are built on the notion of property. There is no undoing history at this point, not in human time at least. Once landed, humans forget. Once landed, greed ensues, and human empathy withers in the intoxication with power over one's property and the necessity for its protection. It's a paradox, as without a notion of property in the person, we cannot be politically free.

When I read in Genesis, "Go towards you, from your land, from your birth, from your father's house, towards the land that I will show you," it is not a physical land, but a land of the heart to which I take leave. It's this constant pivoting between the earthly and heavenly Jerusalems—what Saint Augustine called the *civitas terrena* and the *civitas Dei*—that humans are destined to suffer, the violence and devastation of the former (our human imperfections), and the longing for but ultimate impossibility of residing in the latter for any longer than a brief moment. The in-between of spiritual exile is the only land we can inhabit honestly, and that, only dancing with ever-moving feet. The Sufis know this well. They too wander, whirling so as never to be in one place, but nonetheless searching for and

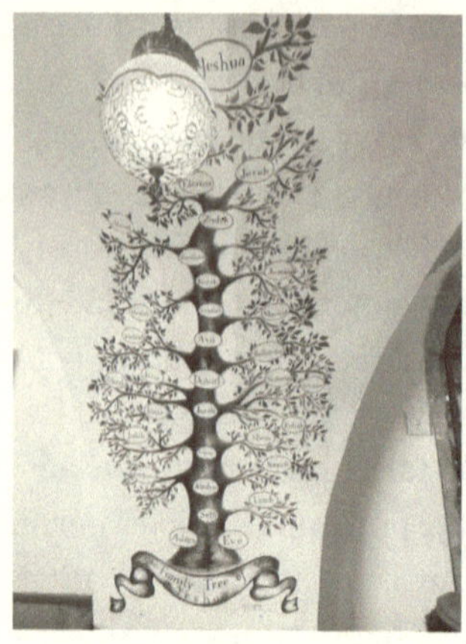


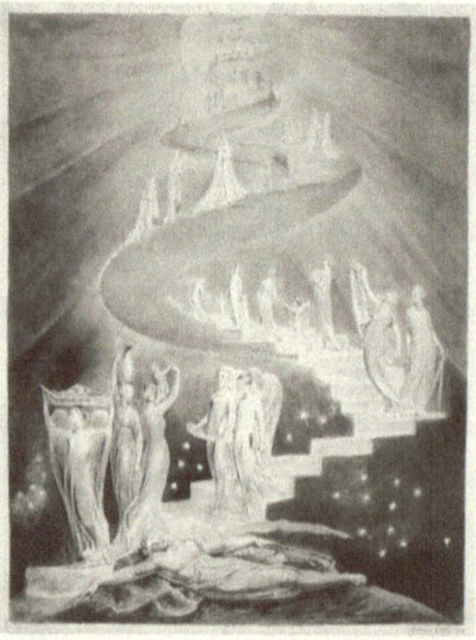

20 The Prophetic Family Tree, on the wall of a café in the Christian Armenian quarter in Jerusalem: "For Christians, as well as Jews and Muslims, Jerusalem is the cosmic tree, its roots in the dirt, its trunk on the earth, its branches stretching upwards into the ether." (Photo: Deborah Kapchan)

21 William Blake, *Jacob's Ladder*. A portrayal of the ladder Jacob saw in his dream, connecting the earthly realm to the heavenly one, the new Jerusalem. (Photo: Open Access)

temporarily finding a center, the cosmic tree, the *axis mundi*, the *barzakh* of the eternal in-between.

Kabir, the fifteenth-century Indian mystic, wrote this:

> Friend, hope for the Guest while you are alive.
> Jump into experience while you are alive.
> Think . . . and think . . . while you are alive.
> What you call "salvation" belongs to the time
> before death.

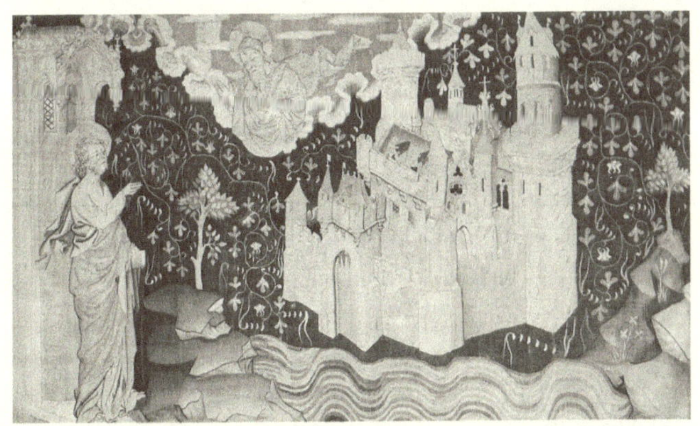

22 The Heavenly Jerusalem, as prophesied in the book of Ezekiel, also called the Promised Land, or Zion, portrayed here in a tapestry from the fourteenth century. (Photo: Open Access)

If you don't break your ropes while you're alive,
do you think ghosts will do it for you after death?

The idea that the soul will join with the ecstatic
just because the body is rotten—
that is all nonsense.
What is found now is found then.
If you find nothing now,
you will simply end up with an empty apartment
in the City of Death.
If you make love with the divine in this life,
in the next life
you will have the face of satisfied desire.

So plunge into the truth, find out who the Teacher is,
believe in the Great Sound!

Kabir says this: When the Guest is being searched for,
it is the intensity of the longing for the Guest
that does all the work.
Look at me, and you will see a slave of that intensity.

# ACKNOWLEDGMENTS

I am grateful to all those who have nourished this work—those named within (my ancestors, family, and friends) and those who wished to remain anonymous. Small details have been changed to protect privacy. My thanks to Margret Grebowicz, who recognized this book before it was born, to Elizabeth Ault at Duke University Press for her encouragement, to Jim Klosty for buoying me these many years, and to Charles Siebert, whose conversations and editorial eye helped it along.

# BIBLIOGRAPHY

Augé, Marc. *Non-Places: An Introduction to an Anthropology of Supermodernity*. Translated by John Howe. London: Verso, 1992.

Bergson, Henri. "Testament." 1937. Quoted in Francis Guiral, "Bergson, Penseur de l'expérience spirituelle: L'humain au-delà de lui-même," *Études: Revue de Culture Contemporaine*, no. 4220 (October 2015). Accessed February 12, 2025. https://www.revue-etudes.com/article/bergson-penseur-de-l-experience-spirituelle/17094.

Blake, William. "Jerusalem." In "*Milton a Poem*, copy B object 2." *The William Blake Archive*, edited by Morris Eaves, Robert N. Essick, and Joseph Viscomi. Accessed February 12, 2025. https://www.blakearchive.org/images/milton.b.p2.100.jpg.

Bly, Robert. *The Kabir Book: Forty-Four of the Ecstatic Poems of Kabir; Versions by Robert Bly*. Boston: Beacon, 1971.

Chouraqui, André. *Lettre à un ami Arab.* Paris: Maison Mame, 1969.

Crapanzano, Vincent. *The Hamadsha: A Study in Moroccan Ethnopsychiatry*. Berkeley: University of California Press, 1973.

Douglas, Mary. *Purity and Danger*. London: Routledge and Kegan Paul, 1966.

Merton, Thomas, and Zhuangzi. *The Way of Chuang Tzu: A Personal and Spiritual Interpretation of the Classic Philosopher of Taoism*. New York: Hyperion, 1995.

Neruda, Pablo. *Residence on Earth, and Other Poems*. Translated by Angel Flores. Norfolk, CT: New Directions, 1946.

Rūmī, Jalāl al-Dīn Muḥammad. "Be Lost in the Call." Translated by Kabir Helminski. Accessed February 12, 2025. https://allpoetry.com/Be-Lost-In-The-Call. Original Persian in *Kolliyat-e Shams: Divan*, edited by Badi'-ozzaman Forouzanfar. Tehran: Hermes, 2022.

Serres, Michel. *Malfeasance: Appropriation Through Pollution?* Stanford, CA: Stanford University Press, 2010.

Skali, Faouzi. *La Voie Soufie*. Paris: Albin Michel, 1985.

Winterson, Jeanette. *The Passion*. New York: Grove, 1997.

www.ingramcontent.com/pod-product-compliance
Lightning Source LLC
La Vergne TN
LVHW051007080826
845145LV00009B/2505